The Rabbi on Forty-seventh Street

Books by Ann Birstein

Star of Glass
The Troublemaker
The Sweet Birds of Gorham
Summer Situations
Dickie's List
American Children
The Rabbi on Forty-seventh Street

The
RABBI
on
FORTY~ SEVENTH STREET

The Story of Her Father by
Ann Birstein

The Dial Press
New York

Published by
The Dial Press
1 Dag Hammarskjold Plaza
New York, New York 10017

"The Congo" from *Collected Poems* by Vachel Lindsay. © 1914 by Macmillan Publishing Co., Inc. Renewed 1942 by Elizabeth C. Lindsay Quoted by permission.
"My Mother's Eyes" by L. Wolfe Gilbert and Abel Baer © 1928, renewed 1956 by Leo Feist, Inc. All rights reserved. Used by permission.
"Shine on Harvest Moon" by Nora Bayes and Jack Norworth © 1908 (renewed by Warner Brothers, Inc.) All rights reserved. Used by permission.
"Some of These Days" by Shelton Brooks. Printed by permission of the copyright owner, Jerry Vogel Music Co., Inc., 58 West 45th St., New York, New York.

Parts of this book appeared in a different form in
CONFRONTATION, Fall 1974; and MADEMOISELLE,
November 1955, under the title "The Voter."

My special thanks to the YIVO Institute for Jewish Research,
and to the MacDowell Colony.

Manufactured in the United States of America
First printing
Design by Francesca Belanger

Library of Congress Cataloging in Publication Data

Birstein, Ann.
The rabbi on Forty-seventh Street.

1. Birstein, Bernard, 1892–1959. 2. Rabbis—New
York (N.Y.)—Biography. 3. New York (N.Y.)—Biography.
I. Title.
BM755.B573B57   296.8′32′0924 [B]   81-17456
ISBN 0-385-27429-7   AACR2

For my father, Rabbi Bernard Birstein

אור זרע לצדיק ולישרי-לב שמחה

Author's Note

Like many Jews of my generation, I understand Yiddish but read it haltingly. Like many Jewish women of any generation, I know less about Orthodox ritual than I ought to because for the most part I wasn't included in it. As to family history, my father, like many Jews of *his* generation, had a weak sense of secular chronology.

These were some of the difficulties involved in writing this book. Among the many joys were conversations with people who knew my father, and the wonderful books I consulted for background information. I am particularly indebted to *Life Is with People* by Mark Zborowski and Elizabeth Herzog, *The Golden Tradition* by Lucy S. Dawidowicz, the Soncino Bible, and Roman Vishniac's *Polish Jews,* whose photographs are unfailingly beautiful and evocative. But mostly I worked with memories, memories of things that happened during my lifetime, and memories of stories I used to hear.

It was a block straight out of Street Scene, *that part of Forty-seventh Street between Eighth and Ninth where I grew up, and looking back I'm often tempted to describe my early years as a Times Square childhood, or even a Hell's Kitchen childhood, just for the sheer drama of the thing. But in fact it was neither. Just a matter of being a little Jewish girl in a neighborhood of pretty hostile Gentiles, though to look at, the street always did have a kind of sweet stage-set quality to it, with the red-brick quiet of Hopper's Sunday Morning, or maybe Dublin, and exactly one of everything to make it complete and self-contained.*

For example, if you started at the northwest corner of Eighth Avenue across the street from the large Automat, where on the schooldays when my mother couldn't have me home, I used to have lunch for a quarter—a vegetable plate because I was kosher: peas, mashed potatoes, Harvard beets, which I regarded as terribly elegant and Ivy League and still do, plus chocolate milk and chocolate cream pie, all eaten at a table reserved for Ladies Only— if you started at this corner, the first thing you would run into would be Professor Mazocchi's Spaghetti Parlor. Truly so called. Inside, as a quick squint through the window revealed, it was white and tiled and kind of sawdusty, like an operating room. Outside, the words Spaghetti Parlor *on the glass, and in the lower right-hand corner in small letters of gold,* Prof. Mazocchi, Prop. *How you can be a professor of spaghetti is a question I ask myself now, though never then. It was too exotic a place for me, such a kosher child—meat sauce!—though Professor Mazocchi himself was a very nice, kind man, and no more exotic when he came out to air himself in his white apron than my uncles.*

I think there was also a village, or street, idiot who emanated from a grocery store somewhere in the region of that corner, and to whom I hope we were not as mean as we probably were. On the other side of the street was a little red fire station like a fire station in a children's book, and beyond, back on the Professor Mazocchi side, an enormous Gothic structure with yards and turrets, P.S. 17. Then a small synagogue, then a brownstone housing Columbia Stage Lighting and a rehearsal hall—often on Yom Kippur, in the interstices between prayers, we would hear the tap dancers dancing in a heavy and unsteady rhythm, a chorus of clumping Ruby Keelers watching their feet—

and farther down, the Sixteenth Precinct, straight out of the turn of the century, a place for Bulldog Drummond, with two white globes that said "16" and an air of being shrouded by night fog and mystery. This is where we all used to walk a little faster.

In between such landmarks, there were many old houses with women leaning on pillows on their windowsills talking down into the street, and kids playing "double Dutch" on the sidewalk with two jump ropes. Tenements and railroad flats, though some of our friends on this block and farther west lived in their own one-family houses, not town houses, just solidly ugly old brownstones. At Succoth, a harvest festival, they were able to build their own succas right in their own backyards. The biblical injunction is that on the festival of Succoth you're not allowed to take your meals anyplace else, and for those without backyards there was a succa on the roof of the synagogue, decorated with fruits and leaves. Then, just to finish up, there was old man Kelly's candy store on the corner, and beyond, in the fruit store world of Ninth Avenue, St. Malachy's Church; the Polyclinic Hospital, where they brought the Nazi, Max Schmeling, after his fight with Joe Louis; Hartley House, which we were not allowed to join because it was a Catholic settlement house; a Greek Orthodox church; a public library on Tenth Avenue, where it was worth a kid's life to go and return a couple of books; and on the side streets, an assortment of pimps, longshoremen, and whores.

It's time, I suppose, to explain what we were doing on Forty-seventh Street in the first place. The fact is that my father was the rabbi of that small synagogue sandwiched

{xiii}

in between Columbia Stage Lighting and P.S. 17, but no ordinary rabbi and of no ordinary synagogue. The shul was called "The Actors Temple" and he was Orthodox, which made him an Orthodox theatrical rabbi. We had to live close by simply because he couldn't ride to work on the sabbath. So there we were, a family of seven, mother, father, four girls, and a boy, a block away from Broadway for religious reasons.

My father was the perfect rabbi for an actors synagogue. Born in 1892 in the Russo-Polish border town of Brest Litovsk and educated at the Slobodka yeshiva, a Lithuanian seminary of great repute, my father was very like an actor himself. Handsome, witty, dapper. He wore a chesterfield coat with a velvet collar and had two canes, one for every day, an amber-handled one for evening. Tiny. Everybody called him the little rabbi, or Rab, and everybody knew why. Except my mother, who was four feet, nine and a half, and said that she always wanted to marry a tall man and thought she had. My father loved theater people and they loved him back, not actors of the legitimate stage particularly, who tended to be lofty and remote and assimilated, but the vaudeville types and radio stars, also prizefighters and ballplayers. He was never rough on them, never made them feel guilty about coming to shul less often than they might have, never chided them for having forgotten all the Hebrew they had learned so painfully for their bar mitzvahs.

It was on Yom Kippur, of course, that the show business world came to us in full force, "famous celebrities," on whom we in the Ladies Balcony, my mother, my three sisters, and I, looked down with awe. But the truly awesome sight was my father on the bima, addressing God as he was directly, in his long white robe and square white yar-

mulke and his ankle-length tallis with the silver-brocaded collar, hands upraised, imploring. It was always a shock to see him dressed in street clothes afterward, greeting the members of his congregation as they filed out the door: Eddie Cantor, if he was in town, Sophie Tucker, Jack Benny, Milton Berle, Oscar Levant, Red Buttons, a young Frank Sinatra, whom someone had invited along. "Gut yom tov," my father would say, "gut yom tov." And I would think—from the Slobodka yeshiva to Broadway.

I
BERIL

I tend to see the yeshiva as all of life, Mont-Saint-Michel,
perhaps, rising from its own pinnacle, or else a large hotel
in the Catskills made of green and brown wood. Probably
it was neither. Probably it was a solemn gray stone building like a YMHA. Finally, I opt for an indeterminate,
sprawling wooden structure and put it on a side street in
Slobodka, mired in the famous mud, the Slobodka *bloteh*.
"At the start of summer and winter," writes a former student, "furtive shadows sidle by; emaciated young bodies,
torn from their mothers' arms, are sent here to study Torah. They hasten, these Jewish youngsters, from the

Kovno side of the bridge to the Slobodka yeshiva. They will remain here always. For the Old Man of Slobodka (the Rabbi Nathan Zevi Hirsh Finkel) said, 'The bridge between Kovno and Slobodka was built to go from Kovno to Slobodka, but not back.' "

As it happens, hardly anyone in town knew Rabbi Finkel. He lived in seclusion apart from his family, and could pass virtually unnoticed, dressed as a poor ordinary shopkeeper, except for the long ultra-Orthodox strands of beard tucked into the collar of his shirt. Even the students rarely saw him. But it was to the Old Man's famous and forbidding center of learning that my father came at the age of nine. Not torn from his mother's arms: that had already happened. His father, a shochet, a ritual slaughterer, had died of blood poisoning, and his mother had boarded him out with a melamed's family in Brest Litovsk, where he had been half starved and beaten into learning his lessons. Hardly the happiest of situations, but what else was the widowed mother of a large brood to do with her youngest orphan?

Possibly the Slobodka yeshiva, which now he was of an age to attend, came as an improvement. Certainly there were no more beatings—it was enough that one of little Beril's ears still rang and was deaf from the rebbe's cuffings. But long hours bent over lecterns, nights sleeping on the hard wooden benches in the study house, the *beth hamedresh*, and of course a perpetual state of semistarvation, alleviated only on those "eating days" when one of the more charitable Jews of the town took him in for a meal. In this manner he learned his Torah, his Gemara, his Mishna, memorized the dimensions of Solomon's Temple to a cubit, debated the ethics of man-to-man dealings in business, considered the loopholes in the divorce laws, and the rules governing connubial behavior during menstruation. By the time he was nineteen and about to be ordained, he had so distinguished himself in all these areas that Rabbi Finkel had emerged from seclusion and taken him personally under his wing, studying and praying with him far into the night, and even arranging a few extra "eating days" so that Beril would not faint dead away before morning. He was also fortunate in that whereas some of his classmates had turned hunchbacked over those lecterns, he was only a bit stoop-shouldered, slight from hunger but not emaciated, dependent on his horn-rimmed glasses but not half-blind. Of course, there was also the added complication that when and if he should survive his studies intact, he would face being inducted into the czar's army. But this was not a dilemma that a yeshiva boy could expect his illustrious mentor to solve, and so Beril had written to his favorite brother in America for two hundred dollars to buy him off.

Meanwhile, as he confidently awaited an answer, an early spring had come to Slobodka. The muck and slime were thick and slippery underfoot but it was spring nevertheless. On his way to the home of Mordecai, the carpenter, for a bowl of kasha, Beril paused and looked toward the Kovno-Slobodka bridge, listening to the occasional twitter of a bird, perceiving a tiny bud on the branch of a naked tree. Soon, on the other side of the Neiman River, woods would turn green, valleys flower, distant blue hills beckon. He had seen this with his own eyes, for in this respect Rabbi Finkel was mistaken. A yeshiva boy *could* cross over the bridge, and Beril had done so a few times over the years, once stopping to listen to the choir music coming from a painted Russian Orthodox church below, once planting his good ear against a classroom door in the

Kovno *gymnasium,* curious to hear what the Gentiles studied. He knew only enough Russian to catch the general drift, but they had seemed to be discussing science and mathematics, subjects not taught at the yeshiva, but not frowned on in certain Orthodox quarters, either. Another time he had chanced on a little band of Yiddish actors performing in the courtyard of an inn, a biblical play about Shulamith and Absalom, that was not unlike a Purim spiel. Of these adventures he had told no one at the yeshiva but confided them to his brother Cathrael far off in America. In return Cathrael, who had settled in Virginia, told him about the great Jamestown exposition he had seen, and of the carved Japanese chest he had bought there in pieces, reassembling it before his skeptical wife at home. Why such a gentle man and skilled artisan had married a *yenta* like Fredel, Beril could never understand. But he had been too young at the time to have his mother or older brothers explain it to him.

Tearing his eyes from the distance and realizing how hungry he was, Beril stamped off mud and ooze, and entered Mordecai's house. A hovel, really, with a rough-hewn wooden table in the center. Spoon in hand, Mordecai already sat waiting for him, ready to be amused and entertained in return for his weekly donation. His wife added another spoon and then retreated. In traditional fashion Beril averted his eyes, but not before he had seen the wife, Rivka, throw him a quick mischievous smile. Behind her, two marriageable daughters giggled.

"*Sholem aleichem,* Beril," Mordecai said, as Beril settled down.

"*Aleichem sholem.*"

"*Nu,* what do you have to tell me today?"

Beril picked up his spoon, hunger forcing him to smile

at Mordecai's scraggly bearded countenance and warty nose. The man even had hair growing out of his ears.

"Well," Beril said, clearing his throat and dipping in, "as we concluded last week, to love God is not enough. A man must also love his fellow man."

"So?" Mordecai said, already deep into his own side of the kasha bowl where the rivulets of chicken shmaltz swam the deepest.

"So this is the teaching of Rabbi Israel Salanter, of whom you no doubt have heard. The great Musar scholar."

Mordecai nodded curtly, gobbling away.

"Of this rabbi," Beril continued, as usual trying to match him spoon for spoon, "it's said that one Kol Nidre night he failed to appear at the synagogue. When the congregation asked him why, he said that on his way to services he heard an infant crying, and that when he went inside the house to see what was wrong, he found that it couldn't reach its bottle." Beril took a few swallows. "What had happened was that the little sister who had been left to mind the baby when the mother went to shul had fallen asleep. So he stayed to mind the baby until the mother came home."

"Why?" Mordecai asked, moving all the soft yellow shmaltz over to his side.

"Because," Beril said, attempting to spoon it back, "it's more of a mitzvah to feed the hungry than go to shul and pray."

Mordecai looked dubious.

"Which brings us to the subject of fasting, if not of actual starvation," Beril pointed out. "Did you know that once during a cholera epidemic Rabbi Israel even provided little pieces of sponge cake on Yom Kippur day to be used if necessary? Though he himself did not partake of any, naturally."

"Naturally."

"The story is probably apocryphal, however," Beril concluded lamely, looking down into the bowl. The word *apocryphal* had not slowed Mordecai's spoon by an inch. Furthermore, the entire river of shmaltz was now collected under his warty nose, and without shmaltz the kasha was almost impossible to swallow. High-pitched girlish giggles emanated from the marriageable daughters in the bedroom alcove, and he knew that Rivka's smile was still trained on him. He thought of Joseph and Potiphar's wife, and then cast about for a more suitable biblical allusion. From Egypt came deliverance.

"Moses!" my father cried.

"Moses?" Mordecai repeated, finally arresting his spoon.

"I'm thinking of the miraculous way in which he parted the Red Sea. . . . Look here, using this kasha and this shmaltz by way of illustration, let's say that there are Pharaoh's soldiers and here are the children of Israel. Right?"

"Right."

"So he parts the waters here to let the soldiers pass. Then brings it all the way over to the other side to drown them. The process is repeated. . . . So . . . and so . . . until all this kasha is covered with the shmaltz."

Beril finished up on his side, a triumph of mind over matter.

"Oy, Beril," Mordecai laughed. "Oy, Beril."

The wife and the daughters laughed even harder.

"I'll see you next Wednesday," Beril sighed. "If we live."

"If we live," Mordecai repeated without rancor, still laughing.

Beril, shivering in his thin coat, left. Outside, all signs of spring had fled. He was also still starving, and there were no more eating days until Friday. He made his slippery, slogging way back to the yeshiva. Sounds of chanted prayer came through the candle-lit windows. Fortunately, just as despair and hunger were gnawing in tandem at his insides, another student, equally woebegone, handed him a letter. The age of miracles had truly not passed. It was from his brother, Cathrael. He read a few lines, then sat down heavily on a bench in the *beth hamedresh*.

"*Dear, beloved young brother,*" Cathrael wrote. "*Legends to the contrary, American streets are not paved with gold. Where do you expect me to find two hundred dollars? I'm already sending home as much as I can. May I remind you that our sainted mother barely has enough to eat, that our twin sisters are still unmarried, that Shlomo is trying to save up to emigrate, and that Hershel is still not right from having been hit over the head when he was sent to dig trenches. I wouldn't bother Yankel, if I were you. He has his own family here to think of.*" Wasn't Beril family too, here or there? "*Besides, a bit of army service might do you good. The world of the yeshiva doesn't seem to satisfy you completely.*"

Hunger yielded totally to despair, never mind that despair was a sin. *Shema Yisroel!* Had Cathrael gone mad? Didn't he know that Jews cut off a finger or foot just to escape this "bit" of army service? Or maybe the fishwife Fredel was behind it. The more he thought about it, the more he thought this must be the case. Desperate ideas seized hold of him. He would emigrate to Palestine and there await the Messiah. . . . He would join a band of traveling actors and . . . At that moment the Old Man, Rabbi Finkel, entered, back from an anonymous perambulation in town, and brought him to his senses. Beril watched him mount the stairs to his silent celibate chamber, hat back on his head, foot-long beard still tucked into his frayed and shabby collar. Could he perhaps consult this spiritual father, this ascetic, about a mundane matter like conscription, tell him of the dereliction of a brother? *Avinu malkeynu,* Beril thought, calling to mind the prayer, Our Father, Our King. As always he tried to remember his real father and couldn't, except for one dim recollection of being carried to his first day of cheder at the age of three, wrapped in a great white tallis.

"Marriage, Beril, marriage," the Old Man said. "You're already nineteen. I was married right after my bar mitzvah."

All very well. But to whom, when, and where? Mordecai's wife and daughters might be beautiful and willing, but to be the poor carpenter's son-in-law would mean to subsist on dry kasha for the rest of his life. And when had such a *kaptsn* ever seen two hundred dollars? "Rebbe—?" But the Old Man had already forgotten the matter entirely and was swaying away ecstatically in prayer. Beril joined him and forgot the matter too, until the next morning when he sent off another letter to Cathrael and this time received an answer only too clearly inspired by Fredel:

There was a fine young woman named Basha Friedlander, it seemed, who lived in the vicinity of Brest Litovsk. No great beauty, perhaps, and an orphan, and possibly a few years older than Beril. But of a fine background, and moreover the soul of piety. In addition, she had rich relatives in the Georgia of America, who besides contributing to the passage would help support the young couple in style. If Beril was interested, and didn't look for the moon, as he was advised not to . . . A meeting was arranged through his mother, Slova, and Beril traveled to Brest Litovsk to get a look at his possible intended. A first glance in the little room behind his mother's tiny grocery told him that his sister-in-law had been true to her word. Basha Friedlander, escorted by a cousin, was certainly no moon. Dark-haired, skinnier than he, she stared at him through similar horn-rimmed glasses. Her dress was dark purple with a black velvet border around the hem and vertical black velvet insets on the bosom. There was a trace of gray in her hair, and she looked to be nearer thirty than twenty. But her smile was gentle, if anxious, and she responded to all of Slova's questions quietly, and even nodded to all of Slova's advice about the care and feeding of Beril, though Slova had been sending Beril into states of semistarvation his entire life. Slova was satisfied. Hershel and Shlomo laughed at the idea of their little brother being a bridegroom. The twin sisters, still unwed, were glumly silent. At his mother's urging, Beril signed the engagement contract and returned to Slobodka to be ordained.

The ordination was more exciting than the betrothal. The Old Man asked him probing questions and so did rabbis and scholars from miles around. They sat in a large dark candle-lit room with cracked and peeling leather-bound volumes lining the walls. When it was over, the Old Man presented him with his ordination paper, his *smicha*. Rabbi to rabbi, he shook hands with his elders, barely suppressing his tears when it came to the Old Man, and then returned to Brest Litovsk to be united with Basha Friedlander under a small canopy held by his brothers. His widowed mother, wearing ruby earrings, the only unsold remains of her dowry, reminded him that the twin sisters still needed husbands, and then he and Basha spent the night in the little room behind the mother's tiny grocery where they had met, Beril having read and reread all the minute regulations regarding this occasion. Basha seemed to have studied them too. Afterward, two strangers, they looked at each other through horn-rimmed glasses, and the next day started out for Bremen where they would wait in an immigrant shed for several weeks for a ship to carry them to their new life. Herded with hundreds of others into steerage, they voyaged in misery and joy. The sailors considered them all dogs. "Beril," a dark and hollow-eyed Basha said, halfway across the Atlantic, "I think I'm pregnant." Smiling enthusiastically, Beril then heard a little knell of doom, rather like those far-off foreign church bells. Nineteen and a rabbi was one thing. But nineteen and a father? "Maybe it's only seasickness," he told Basha, holding her head on the wet windy deck. One day he looked up to see land. Enter America. The golden land. The *goldene medina*.

But first, of course, there was Ellis Island. Sitting beside his nauseated wife in the great caged reception hall, surrounded by bags and bundles, my father congratulated himself on having already learned two English words: *trachoma* and *tuberculosis*. Which, it turned out, after three days of being poked and prodded, having their chests thumped and listened to, and their eyelids lifted with button hooks, he and Basha were free of. He had expected her to brighten up at the news, but she seemed darker and dimmer than ever, almost as if she wanted to be sent back. He himself, now that their detention was almost over, felt lively and alert, homesick for the old world, but curious as to what life in the new would hold for him. So far things were looking good. Cathrael had scraped up the twenty-five dollars they needed to enter the country; another brother, Yankel, would meet them on shore; Basha's uncle, a shochet like his dead father, was waiting to set them up in Atlanta.

"Truly *di goldene medina,*" Beril remarked to a bearded old man sitting next to him.

"*Vos?*"

"Especially when you understand *goldene* to refer not only to money, but freedom and opportunity."

"Do you know where is Brooklyn?" the old man said.

"Brooklyn!" Beril exclaimed. "My brother Yankel lives there," and was about to continue except that they were all now being herded out by a member of the Hebrew Immigrant Aid Society. Section by section, they boarded a gray wooden ferry and sailed across the choppy New York Harbor, glimpsing the Statue of Liberty. On shore there was bedlam. People stooped and kissed the earth, women wept, babies wailed, relatives embraced new-found relatives. Amid this tumult Beril could not find Yankel, though he was armed with a recent photograph. "Excuse me," he asked the man from HIAS, "but this is a picture of my brother, Yankel the tailor. If you could—" And then in that instant spied his oldest brother, standing dour and apart, the lone member of the Beril-Basha delegation. Beril embraced him passionately. They kissed on the lips. "And the wife?" Beril said, having presented Basha. "Busy with the children," Yankel said. "What do you think? There's time to waste in America?" Shaking his head and looking at his pocket watch, Yankel helped them pick up their bags and bundles. Then he led them from one streetcar to another, down into a subway train from which they emerged shaken and rattled to take still another streetcar which they rode to the end of the line. After all of it, Yankel's small shabby set of rooms was not unlike those in the old country, except that there was perhaps a little bit more furniture. A few *landslayt* and relatives had crowded in to greet them, and unidentified children scrambled underfoot. Yankel's wife, as dour as her husband, gave them tea, schnapps, dry cakes, sponge cakes, herring. It did not seem the place to ask about freedom and opportunity.

Beril and Basha were to stay a few days, sharing a bedroom with three of Yankel's children. As Beril made the rounds of the guests, exchanging news of marriages, pogroms, sickness and births, the terrible Beilis case in which a Jew had been accused of ritual murder, Basha stood apart from a group of chattering women, nervously fingering her wedding ring, and on the next thin finger a gold ring with a dark green stone which Slova had given her. She wore a black dress and high-laced black shoes and looked as if she were in mourning. Later that night, when the tumult had subsided but he was still excited by the arrival, Beril wanted to, but Basha said no, indicating the three children sleeping in the next bed. She often said no, even when there were no children. But perhaps she was right. The children were stirring. He thought of the life ahead, and what kind of rabbinical post the uncle would find him in Georgia. Then he tried to look out the window but couldn't see beyond it. They were facing a narrow courtyard and the tenement next door blocked out the view.

In the morning, after a quick bout with his phylacteries, Yankel hung a tape measure around his neck, told his young brother where the shul was, and hurried off to the tailor shop where he worked. Fortunately, the shul was easy to find, just down the street, a little wooden building, and like Yankel's apartment, familiar and full of *landslayt*. "Old man Finkel?" the rabbi in charge said. "Who doesn't know about Finkel of Slobodka?" and introduced Beril all around as a marvel, a full-fledged rabbi at such a tender age. The other men crowded about, asking him probing questions, teasing him a bit, and my father passed with flying colors, giving as good as he got, but deliberately holding back a bit out of respect, and contributing a few new nasal melodies to old prayers. Afterward, a landsman escorted Beril to a travel bureau to make arrangements for the trip to Georgia. Many other would-be travelers stood on long lines at the counters amid much noise and commotion. Was there no respite in this country from crowds and commotion? Posters beckoned him to foreign lands, although he was already in one. Only one picture interested him, strangely, of Florida, a place called the Everglades. It showed a swamp with hanging trees and beautiful flowers. He turned away uneasily, filled with odd intimations, and later when he returned to Yankel's apartment, tickets in hand, did not mention it to Basha. Exotic foliage was not in her line. Neither, for he had tried it, was the Song of Songs.

At mid-week they boarded the train, assisted by Yankel's brother-in-law. How busy everyone was in America! The wheels steamed up. They arranged themselves not in a compartment, but in a long carriage where all passengers were equal. Beril realized that he had seen nothing of New York but Ellis Island and the Statue of Liberty. Brooklyn was a forgettable congested blur. Then trees and trees and more trees sped by. In the morning, a dusky dawn, shanties, and Negroes working in the fields. "Look, Basha, look!" She put down her Yiddish prayer book and gazed at him inquiringly over her eyeglasses. By the end of twenty-seven hours of sitting in one place, he was writhing to get where he was going, and Basha was still murmuring over her prayers.

The station in Atlanta was soaked with sun, the air balmy. They stood on the open platform, sweating in their heavy clothes. Soon a little boy, identifying himself as the son of Basha's uncle, came along, trundling a cart into which they loaded their possessions. Well, so much for Fredel's prattle about fine servants and livery. They followed the child across wooden streets to the uncle's house, where the uncle, a stout man with a blond beard and a square skullcap, emerged into the bright sunlight to greet them. His long black gabardine was shiny. His strong blunt hands were made for wielding knives. The garden where they stood was overgrown and ragged, the peeling white house behind rose from a sagging porch. For a moment they all waited unsmiling, as if they were posing for a photograph. Then the uncle's wife appeared, shooing out several children, who scampered off into the scraggly bushes with their brother, abandoning the wagon and possessions in the front yard. There was a sudden spate of hugging and kissing, and Beril and the uncle kissed too, sensibly and seriously, taking each other's measure. The uncle's wife finally wiped her eyes with a corner of her apron, Basha dabbed under her glasses with a small handkerchief taken from her sleeve, and they all proceeded into the house, passing a company parlor with velvet and horsehair furniture, white glass lamps, velvet portieres, and a picture of an old *zayde* hanging by a tassel, and settled down in the kitchen. It was very hot. Food stewed and simmered on the black coal stove, the wooden table was laden with buttermilk, cakes, fruit, herring, and a bottle of schnapps. "And so, Beril," the blond uncle said after they had eaten a bit, smacking his lips and wiping his bearded mouth with the back of his hand. Such red lips. "How do you like it here in America?" "Well," Beril began with a smile, "to come as a stranger to the Promised Land is also to wonder how to enter . . ." The uncle nodded. "The sages further tell us . . ." The women retreated and, as the sages grew in number, carried bundles up the back stairs. "Or, as the Psalmist concludes . . ."

The uncle and Beril themselves concluded with two glasses of schnapps, and the uncle nodded again, giving the impression that he would quote from the little discourse later on, giving credit where credit was due, and receiving a bit of his own into the bargain. For the moment, however, he seemed to have taken the floor.

"Beril, I like you."

"Thank you, Uncle."

"I can see that you're lively, intelligent, and not bad to look at."

"Thank you, Uncle."

"So I've decided to make you my assistant."

"Your *assistant*?" Beril said.

"Don't worry. You'll be able to pay off the railroad ticket from your wages."

"But, Uncle, I thought—"

"We have a growing Jewish population here, you see. We have three kosher butchers. We've built a new shul and even got a new rabbi from Canton, Ohio. Lekhem. A holy man, a *tsadik*. His former congregation gave him a black umbrella with a silver handle as a going-away present."

"A silver-handled umbrella," Beril repeated, impressed in spite of himself.

"We'd better go along now and see him," the uncle said, adding proudly in English, "Atlanta is *booming*."

Booming. English words had such a peculiar sound. Well, to it then in this booming Atlanta. The shochet business would not last long, anyway. Within a few months he would pay off this debt which he had not known to be a debt, and find himself a new position. Beril and the uncle washed their hands, pouring water from a pitcher over their fingertips, lightly sang a few words of benediction, thrust on their jackets, the uncle's covering a striped shirt with black suspenders, and set off to see the *tsadik* from Canton, Ohio. The rabbi's wife received them formally and ushered them into a company parlor like the uncle's, where they sat stiff as ramrods on a horse-hair sofa, staring at starched lace curtains, until they were shown into the rabbi's study. Heavy portieres covered the windows. All was calm, tranquil, meditative. The rabbi sat behind his desk, a heavy leather-bound, flaking tome open before him, leaning on one elbow, studying it over his wire-rimmed glasses. For a moment, Beril imagined he saw the Old Man. This one too was a legend and, according to the uncle, studied thirteen hours a day, deploring how much he had still to learn, and praying to God for strength and guidance. In between he had managed to squeeze in four sons and four daughters. He rose to greet them, shook hands, then motioned them to seats, though he himself remained standing, hands behind his back as he asked about the trip, the arrival. A perfect patriarch with pink cheeks and a snowy white long beard. His smile as he looked at Beril was kind, his eyes kind too, but curious and searching.

"Your uncle tells me you studied at the Slobodka yeshiva?"

"And was ordained there," my father added quickly.

"By Rabbi Finkel?"

"Yes. Do you know him?"

"We were students together," Rabbi Lekhem said, smiling. "Many years ago. . . . Oy, that Slobodka *bloteh*. . . ."

Beril waited for the rabbi to continue his reminiscences, or else to ask a few searching questions to which he would respond with all his yeshiva wit and learning, while the uncle listened silently, impressed by how Beril comported himself. But the rabbi seemed lost in a dream, and even returned to his tome and leafed through a few pages before he looked up and remembered his visitors.

"Oh, yes," he said, rising and ushering them to the door. "Until tomorrow, then."

"Tomorrow?" Beril said.

"That's when the committee will examine you."

"I'm ready to be examined now."

"Tomorrow," the rabbi repeated gently, giving Beril another slightly quizzical smile before he returned to his books. The rabbi's wife showed them out, handing the uncle pastries wrapped in a napkin for the children. Outside, Beril stood a moment, blinking in the sunlight. America?

The examination went well. There was never any doubt of its outcome. He came with his father's case containing two knives and a whetstone, knowing to a hair how sharp the blades must be, how to tell at a glance a diseased chicken from a well one, precisely where the unkosher hindquarters of a cow began and left off. Afterward, there was general rejoicing, with the rabbi and the committee members congratulating him. At home, the aunt prepared a feast fit for shabbos, and Basha threw her arms around him with an unnerving girlish glee, not knowing, or maybe not caring to know, that any bright young seminarian could have answered the committee's questions off the top of his head. All through the chopped liver, the chicken soup with knaidlach, the roast chicken, the noodle pudding, the sliced cucumbers from the garden, the honey cake, he sat silently, tasting only a morsel here and there, thinking of the stench of the slaughter shed, the blood, and cattle lowing, death by blood poisoning. He watched the children stabbing their food, heard the uncle rebuke them with pride, glanced at the mysterious mound of Basha's stomach, and reminded himself that children were a blessing. "Such a *balebosteh* you are, *tante*," Basha said, serving from behind, noticing her husband's lack of appetite. "You'll be one too," the *tante* assured her, observing Beril also.

Assisted by an older girl in a pinafore and long braid down her back, the two women did the dishes, whispering together a bit, and so to bed. Beril and Basha went upstairs before the aunt and uncle, Basha following him with a wistful glance over her shoulder toward the warmth of the kitchen. Upstairs, in the tiny attic room, a brass bed piled high with a comforter and down pillows awaited them. Basha, retiring to a dark corner, undressed. Turning his back, Beril did likewise. They performed their ablutions with a pitcher and bowl on the dresser, Beril first as was fitting, and laid their eyeglasses side by side. They climbed into bed, Basha in a long white nightgown, Beril in his long underwear. Outside, a black tree rustled, crickets chirped. A sudden sweet scent filled the room. "What do I smell?" Beril asked. "The *tante* says 'honeysuckle,' " Basha murmured. Honeysuckle. Sighing heavily, he reached out for her.

A house was available, a half house actually, shared by a carpenter whom the uncle knew. Beril had asked Basha to come with him when he looked at it, their first married home. But she had demurred, smiling shyly and insisting that Beril knew best, a right answer that sounded wrong, and stayed behind on the porch with her aunt, shelling peas, and waving good-bye in the heat, still strangely girlish. Accompanied by the uncle, now the authority on everything American, he looked at the place from all angles. It was painted green—green or red, it made no difference; my father was color-blind—a wooden structure of three stories, divided straight down the middle. There were two separate front doors, a picket fence all askew, a weedy garden. Inside, because of the division, the rooms seemed peculiarly dark and narrow. "Never mind," the uncle said, frowning, giving him a nudge, "it's a bargain." Twelve dollars a month for five rooms a bargain? "Beril, you're not in Slobodka." True. He handed over a deposit of three dollars to the carpenter, who said he would give it to the landlord, and watched him exchange glances with the uncle. In return, he was presented with an iron key, which failed to turn the lock. The key was symbolic only, the uncle explained. There was also mysterious talk about cellars and attics. Everything else seemed to be in order, including the cabbage roses on the wallpaper, which the carpenter said would be sure to please the wife. Back at the uncle's porch, Beril bypassed the roses and gave the key to Basha, who also did not know what to do with it. They put it upstairs on top of the bureau, where it sat like a souvenir, alongside the blue velvet bag containing Beril's phylacteries.

In the ensuing days a few sticks of furniture were purchased, also courtesy of a friend of the uncle's—linens they had brought with them from Russia in the form of Basha's dowry, which also included two comforters, six down pillows, and a pair of brass candlesticks—and on moving day they took possession of the half house accompanied by carts, a horse and a wagon, the uncle, aunt, and all their children. Rabbi Lekhem stopped by on his way to shul to bless the bread and salt, the carpenter and his wife dropped in, and there were heartfelt cries of congratulation—"*Mazel tov!*" "*Zol zayn mit glik!*" "*Nor af simchas!*"—followed by a few pious songs. In the midst of the rejoicing, Beril suddenly missed his mother and could not quite figure out why. She had never been much of a mother to him, and yet he wished she were there in her ruby earrings, sharing this moment, weeping at having lived to see this day. He said nothing about it to Basha, an orphan, and by the time he went on to shul with the men the feeling had passed. They were all discussing the sinking of the S.S. *Titanic*, which by coincidence had hit an iceberg on his twentieth birthday, April 15. It was very bad for the Jews. Most of the steerage passengers had gone down with the ship and, in First Class, Isidor Straus and his wife, noted philanthropists and friends to immigrants. In full evening dress, Mrs. Straus had chosen to drown with her husband. "I would rather die with you than live alone," she had said. At home, he found Basha with a rag tied around her head, trying to make order.

Each day he got up at daybreak, took his phylacteries out of the blue velvet bag, and with the little box of these *tfiln* strapped to his forehead, leather thongs wound around his arm, said his prayers, and thanked God for making him a man instead of a woman. Even in the heat of the Georgia summer, he wore *tsitses*, a short tallis, over his flannel undershirt, fringes left hanging and visible. The slaughterhouse stank of flat red blood. The cows moaned. Around noon, he took the streetcar home for a dairy lunch: maybe pot cheese and sour cream with chopped vegetables, maybe a salmon cutlet. (The aunt had shown Basha how to open a can.) Then back to working off the passage money. One day, while he was tackling a cheese blintz, Basha at his shoulder asking if it was all right, a man came to register him for the City Directory. A big-bellied chap with a shiny black suit, watch chain, derby hat, white cotton socks, and black high-laced oxfords. Basha looked terrified. "Go upstairs," he told her. But the man wanted her to stay. For the purposes of "vital statistics." Strange, uncomfortable words that smacked of the czar. And such information the man wanted: births, deaths, other assorted data. Beril cleared his throat to hide his confusion and embarrassment. The fact was that besides being older than he, Basha didn't even have an actual birthday. He offered up his own. "April fifteenth, 1892," he said proudly. Insufficient. "This year on my birthday the *Titanic* sank." Still not enough. Basha was on the verge of tears. Beril glared at her. He had a sense that one false move and it was all up with them. On the other hand, he considered, his Talmudic training coming to the fore, in times of stress wasn't it a mitzvah to put one over on the goyim? Then and there he decided that Basha had been born on May 30, right around Shevuoth, and for good measure made her five years *younger* than he. The tears dried in Basha's widened eyes, though what with the gray streaking her hair she hardly looked like a girl of fifteen. And now what? "Profession?" the derbied man said. "Rabbi." "All Jews tells me they're rabbis. What else?" "Well," Beril began, with a placating smile, "a few cows here, a chicken there, which is to say—" "Sign here." Beril signed, with a flourish—he had been practicing for this moment—and did not realize until another moment had passed that he had been put down as a butcher.

Butcher? What was going on in this country, anyway? Grim and determined, he bought an English language newspaper, *The Atlanta Constitution,* that very day for a few groschen, as he still called his pennies, and settled down with it right after supper. To tell the truth, he didn't even know what a City Directory was, and had no one to ask without appearing to be too much of a greenhorn—maybe Rabbi Lekhem?—but that could wait. Meanwhile, there was more news than he had imagined. A new president was to be elected in November and the country was being asked to decide between Taft, Roosevelt, and Wilson. Militant-looking American women in

terrible hats were parading around demanding the vote—
he looked up at Basha, who was safely washing the pots—
and Roosevelt said it should be put to a referendum. He
himself would not vote for another ten years, when he
became a citizen, but if it were up to him now, he would
choose Woodrow Wilson, an educated man and a professor. There was also an item that men in high places the
world over were protesting the baseless charges brought
against the Jews in the Beilis case, but this was no real
news. The Yiddish papers were full of it, and it made him
nervous to see the matter discussed in English, so pub-
licly and officially, especially coming as it did on the heels
of the City Directory. He had had enough of pogroms,
beatings, assaults, persecutions for a while. He put the
paper down, resolving that on the day his son was born—
and of course his firstborn would be a son—he would buy
another copy of *The Atlanta Constitution* in his honor.
That way, the boy, named after his father Shmuel Yosef
but an American, would have a *real* birthday.

A few months passed. The slaughterhouse stank even in
colder weather. At home, pregnant Basha seemed quietly
content, marketing with the other women, bargaining
over a few pennies less for a bit of fish or meat, a scrawny
chicken, whose feathers she plucked sitting outside the
chicken lady's coop, since that way it was cheaper. She
also put up pickles, sauerkraut, strawberry preserves, did
the laundry in a big boiling vat on top of the black coal
stove, stirring the clothes with an old broom handle, and
pressing them with a pair of heavy black flatirons which
she made sizzle with a moistened forefinger. Sometimes in
the evenings, while Basha darned or knit, or murmured

in a high thin voice over her Yiddish prayer book, Beril played chess with one of the men from the synagogue, not the uncle, who had no head for the game. He was a good player, impatient when he lost, impatient if the game went slowly, walking around the board and humming little "deedle-deedle-dee" melodies that made his opponent look up nervously. Other evenings he studied with the men in the *beth hamedresh*, under Rabbi Lekhem's guidance. More and more, the rabbi treated him as a son, smiling on him more fondly than upon his four pompous actual sons, not to mention the four stuck-up daughters, surprising him with difficult questions, laughing at his wit, frowning at some minute error in interpreting the Law. Secretly, he nursed the hope that when the stint with the uncle was over, Rabbi Lekhem would have something in mind for him. But what? They were a small congregation, a tiny island of piety in a hostile area, as visible in their strange clothes as the Negroes whom they saw shuffling down the wooden streets in the heat of the day. He did not understand this Negro business. Slaves they no longer were, but not free men either. They sang about Moses. They could not vote even though they were citizens. In public buildings, they had to use separate toilets. Only the Jewish peddlers let them try on clothes before they bought them, or called them Mr. or Mrs. But Atlanta was booming, wasn't it? He was still trying to make friends with that word.

As Basha grew heavier and heavier with child, husband and wife no longer made love. It was unsafe, profane. To Basha, the rebbetzin suggested that in spite of the extra expense they should have two beds, and Basha anxiously carried the suggestion to Beril, who agreed. Nevertheless, the sight of the two beds depressed him, they were so separate, so swamped in the old world bedding. But of course he could not mention the matter to anyone, certainly not Rabbi Lekhem, though as more and more often happened, the two of them studied together privately, sharing moments of intense intellectual illumination by lamplight. In fact, there was so much Beril could not mention to anyone. That he had flirted with the cabala, for instance, then dismissed it as too dangerous for this time and this country. That he was trying to learn Greek. That he was attempting to further improve his English by reading Milton's *Paradise Lost*, which in some ways reminded him of the play about Shulamith and Absalom he had seen as a yeshiva boy. And meanwhile, the High Holidays passed, his first in the new world. It grew colder and colder. My father had no overcoat. He would have liked a fine overcoat. He would have liked to buy one for his wife, with a high fur collar and ruby earrings to dance against it, like his mother's. But as it was, Basha wore an old coat of the uncle's, borrowed from the aunt, to envelop her girth, and Beril turned up the collar of his jacket for a little extra warmth.

One November night, the pains started and then increased in severity. Beril ran out for the midwife, racing against the pounding of his heart. The midwife, an ugly fat hag with a mole and missing teeth, laughed at him, though it was no laughing matter, and ambled along behind him as slowly as a *shvartze*. The aunt and the carpenter's wife soon came. Then more women. There was much fetching and carrying, boiling of water, laying out of baby clothes, lining of a dresser drawer in flannel. Hours passed. Basha had started screaming. He too was in agony, torn by guilt and remorse—to be the instrument of such suffering! Once they let him upstairs. Basha was in much greater anguish than his own, and he didn't know how to help her. He didn't even know which part of the bed to sit on. He wiped her forehead with his handkerchief, squeezed her hand. But Basha moaned in pain, her ring with the dark green stone digging into their joined flesh. He let go. She didn't seem to know him anyway. She was too preoccupied with her contractions, which were coming at quicker and quicker intervals. With an imperious wave of her hand, the ugly midwife sent him away: meaning, now to business.

The business culminated in an infant's sharp cry. Beril raced upstairs, was shooed out again. He waited outside his own bedroom door to gain admittance to his own son. Finally, he was allowed to tiptoe in. The infant was washed and swaddled, held in the crook of Basha's arm. She smiled weakly, and closed her eyes even before he had finished smiling back. He peered down into the tiny red face, then undid the blanket. Were all its particulars in order? Yes, it had ten fingers and ten toes, plus other necessary equipment. (The midwife leered.) Beril was vastly relieved and wondered why. Nobody on either side of the family, to his knowledge, was missing any appendages. Then God be blessed that it hadn't happened this time either. He said the necessary blessings and *brochas,* and was shooed out after one last peek, one last protest. All night on the living-room settee he kept waking, hearing the piercing cry of an infant, but whether in his waking mind or in his sleep he wasn't sure. His son, his son. His kaddish.

* * *

In fact, as far as his household was concerned he might just as well not have existed. In shul, at the naming of the boy, he was called up to the Torah, pelted with candies. At home, the aunt, the carpenter's wife, and sundry other women bustled about, ignoring him. There was endless cooking, endless female laughter. He decided that for the baby's bris, the party would be as lavish as possible, even though it meant going into deeper debt to the uncle. Still in bed, Basha handed over her baby reluctantly for the ceremony, looking at her husband as if he were a distant relative. He was assured that in spite of her apparent frailty, she was strong enough to do it again. More laughter, more jokes. He was tired of jokes about so serious, not to say crushing a matter. Nevertheless, he enjoyed playing host, though Rabbi Lekhem commanded more respect, and the mohel had a stained vest and a most unsanitary beard.

And of course, and as usual, life had to go on. Sometimes, to restore himself, Beril took out *The Atlanta Constitution* of November 20, 1912, which he had bought the day of little Shmuel Yosef's birth. The news, not good to begin with, never looked much better. There was a menacing war in Turkey, and though Woodrow Wilson had won the election, the women in those hats were still demanding the vote. When he first perceived that the pages were turning yellow and the folds had begun to tear, he put it away with his *smicha* and other important papers, inside the City Directory, which now identified him in print and forever, as "Bernard Bernstein, butcher," though the address at least was correct. He bought another *Atlanta Constitution*, and then another, until it became a daily habit to roll it up and place it in his side pocket where it stuck out significantly as he went about his business. At night, he pondered over the hard words as Basha basked in his glory. When the news was especially bad, he said nothing. As had been predicted, she had soon become pregnant again, and he didn't want to mar the new baby.

Nevertheless, a terrible event had come about that could not be kept secret. Right there in Atlanta, a man named Leo Frank, manager of a pencil factory, had been accused of murdering a fourteen-year-old employee, Mary Phagan. Frank had protested his innocence, but southern men had never liked the idea of their women working in factories to begin with, much less one run by a Jew from the North, and feelings ran high. The Yiddish and the English press were full of the matter. A committee was formed, my father among them, to call on Rabbi Lekhem and ask him what to do. The rabbi told them not to meddle. Frank was convicted not only of strangling the girl but of raping her as well, and was sentenced to death. The committee called again, and this time Rabbi Lekhem said he had better go and see Frank in jail himself. It was a brief visit, especially since Leo Frank hadn't wanted the old rabbi to come in the first place. The jailers and the warden were mystified. Why didn't Frank want to see one of his own? Poor Russian Jews *weren't* his own, Frank in his pince-nez, the president of the local B'nai B'rith, explained. Further mystification. Jews were Jews, weren't they? Which was perhaps why, after the visit, the rabbi suggested to his congregation that all girls and women stay at home at night, and go about as little as possible in the daytime. He was smiling kindly as he said this, and assured them that there was nothing to worry about, but nobody argued. The women did their marketing quickly, glancing over their shoulders, collapsing hysterically only when they reached home. The men went to shul in groups. No one was hurt except Beril, and that for the most innocent of all reasons.

What had happened was that one warm shabbos afternoon when things had quieted down a bit, he had decided to take his little Yosele out for a walk in the country, and by mistake had wandered into a dangerous redneck district. A group of idlers, in straw hats tilted back and striped shirts with collar buttons but no collars, were drinking whiskey on a sagging porch. Laughing raucously when they saw the little Jew and his son, they pitched an assortment of objects at the pair, one of which, a jagged sardine can, hit Beril on his upper lip. He stopped and touched the place with his fingers. The fingers came away bloody. The blood incited the rednecks to further laughter. "Kikes!" they called out. "Murderers! Stranglers! Rapists!" and other names Beril didn't understand but caught the gist of. Crying with fright, little Yosele wrapped his arms around his father's leg. Beril tried to detach him with as much dignity as he could muster, but the child hung on for dear life. Thus hobbled, he proceeded to the end of the street, found himself in a dead end, turned around, and slowly and deliberately came back the same way. He had managed to detach Yosele from his leg and now held him firmly by his little upraised hand. This time there were no jeers or catcalls, only astonished silence. "What the *hell*—?" A renewed burst of raucous laughter followed them to the bend in the road, where Beril swooped up his son, and ran.

"But you're *bleeding*," Basha said.

"I know it," Beril said, looking around for the leftover bottle of slivovitz from Pesach. He took a healthy swig, then dabbed some on his upper lip, wincing at the pain.

"But, Beril—"

The little boy looked up at him awed and mute, still terrified beyond speech. Beril gave him a spoonful of honey to lick.

"My God—*raboyne shelolim*—what happened?"

"Be quiet, woman," he commanded her, silent as a stone himself, and went off to shul.

For wasn't it *her* fault that they were all in Atlanta in the first place, her and those famous relatives of hers? He consoled himself that the next one would be another boy, another kaddish, but was out of luck in this too. A few months later Basha gave birth to a girl, Sarah Rachel, named after Basha's mother, dark-haired and with an eye that slipped a little of its own accord. He loved her anyway, his child, never mind that the eye also came from Basha's side of the family. Still, was this South the place to bring up any children?

The Frank case rushed from climax to climax. Banner headlines screamed each development in the news. The Supreme Court had refused to review the case, with Justice Oliver Wendell Holmes dissenting. The governor, convinced of Frank's innocence, had commuted the sentence, and forfeited his own political career. A journalist named Tom Watson wrote inflammatory anti-Semitic broadsides. Testimony was given by a drunken Negro janitor and also by men in high places. Statements were issued, refuted, lofty sentiments expressed. There were rallies, near riots, torchlight parades. Like the Beilis case, and the Dreyfus affair before it, the Frank case had cast ever-widening concentric circles in its own dark pool. Yet it remained a Jewish matter. And at the heart of it, its core, was the little band of Atlanta Jews. Sometimes Beril thought of the word *doom* in this connection, which sounded like but wasn't *boom*.

One night after services, the rabbi suggested that Beril come to his house the next evening, a casual suggestion but with the force of a command. Beril arrived, excited and serious, smoothing the small black mustache which he had grown to cover the sardine-can scar and which, according to Basha, made him look handsomer. The rebbetzin ushered him into the rabbi's study, served them tea with raspberry jam at the bottom of the glasses, and retreated. Of the four sons and overeducated daughters, there was no sign. He and the rabbi spoke of this and that, but not at length—the rabbi was no idle chatterer—just a few inquiries about Beril's family in the old country, the mother, the twin sisters still in need of dowries, the brothers here, the brothers there, young Shmuel Yosef, Basha, the joys of family life in general, though Rabbi Lekhem's own children were brought to him as before a king. All in all, a peculiar overture to a serious discussion of political matters, but it was hard always to know what to expect of a man who studied thirteen hours a day and never saw the sun. In the pause, Beril imagined he saw his cue. The rabbi waited, smiling.

"Well," Beril began, "as the sages have told us . . . and also Emile Zola . . ."

"What Emile Zola?" the rabbi said, awakening as if from a long dream.

"Excuse me, Rabbi, but didn't you—?"

"I was going to tell you about Rome, Georgia."

{ 33 }

This was a new one. Of Rome, Italy, Beril had heard, but Rome, Georgia?

"It's a small community of several thousand souls," Rabbi Lekhem explained, using the old religious term. "But a man could have a good home there, a lot of fresh air for his growing children."

What did fresh air have to do with it? Beril wondered. He didn't like the gist of it, the tone, nor for that matter the old rabbi's increasingly benign smile. Unless—was it possible?—this up-and-coming community needed a young up-and-coming rabbi? Beril Birstein, no, Bernard Birstein, rabbi. It sounded good. He could imagine welcoming Reb Lekhem as a colleague and honored guest, calling him up to the Torah, inviting him to preach a sermon. Their light would reflect on each other. It was not until this point that my father heard, very clearly and distinctly, the word *shochet*. The light went out. Again *shochet*?

"The old one is retiring," Rabbi Lekhem said.

"Why?"

"His hands quiver. The animals are suffering. There have been complaints."

"I see," Beril said, not seeing at all.

"But he'll help you get settled, find you a house."

What was this, a special Yom Kippur, that his fate had already been decided in advance? Beril's jaw clenched. He smoothed his mustache and looked Rabbi Lekhem straight in the eye. But the old man had already risen, shaking hands as on a bargain successfully concluded, unaware that he was in fact a Solomon ignoring the cries of a mother whose child he had just ordered to be cut in half. Fortunately, the rabbi was not a man who expected to be thanked for favors, since he wasn't. At home, Beril sat down at his supper table like a lord of the manor, thinking, threatening little Yosel, when he tried to put his finger in the tsimmes, with a *patsh*. Basha was flabbergasted, such a thing had never happened before. She clutched the wall-eyed baby, Sarah Rachel, to her breast. Beril looked at his family darkly. What was his special connection with this corner of the diaspora that he was being sent into part after part of it? The rabbi had been right about one thing, however. The family was growing. There was now another one in Basha's stomach.

Rome. A year, two years. The debt to the uncle had been repaid, but there were debts to follow, and no way to expunge them except through the bloody business of being a shochet. He was the only one in town, the little backwoods shul not even having a regular rabbi, so that his reputation as a sage and wit grew. But on the one occasion when Lekhem came to preach a guest sermon, the congregation so jockeyed for position at the feast in the old shochet's house afterward, he found himself at the far end of the table like a musician at a wedding. In his Talmudic studies he struggled on alone, and in *Paradise Lost* had finally and reluctantly come to the Expulsion. "The world was all before them, where to choose/Their place of rest," he read pensively, "and Providence their guide. . . ."

For diversion, he was persuaded to join the Masons, Cherokee Lodge, but disliked wearing the apron, and also the Indian connotation. Only *The Atlanta Constitution* kept him in touch with the great outside world, hard to come by as it was, and always late. It told him of the Dolly Sisters, Caruso, baseball, the beginnings of a world war. And then one day that failed him too. There were sketches on the front page, not photographs but vivid enough: one of a man in a pince-nez and a round collar, a proper president of B'nai B'rith, the other of the same man's body hanging from a tree in the night, shirt-sleeved and with neck askew. People with flaming torches jeered at the corpse. Lynched. Another English word. Leo Frank had been lynched. *Enough!* Beril cried in his heart, pounding a fist on the table. "Basha!" he cried aloud. Basha came running, pushing her glasses back onto her nose.

"How is your sister in Chicago?" Beril asked.

"*Oy, vay,*" Basha said, breathing hard. "I thought—my sister in Chicago? She's fine, thank God."

"Good. Write and tell her that we're coming."

"To visit?"

"To stay."

"Beril—*du bist meshuga?*"

In answer, Beril glared at her over his horn-rimmed glasses. She stared back through hers. Again, Beril's word was law. She wrote to her sister, who welcomed them with open arms. The die was cast, they packed, set off, the small community having given them a rousing but puzzled farewell. At the station, Basha, encumbered by the new little soul, Malke Leah, who like her mother also did not have a birthday (Rome had not got around to registering them), let out one more mournful "Oy, Beril." This time he did not command the woman to silence. He shifted the silver-handled umbrella he had bought with his own money from one hand to the other, and told her in plain English to shut up. Steam hissing at its wheels, the train departed. During the whole trip, Malke Leah, unfortunate infant, never stopped squalling and wetting her pants. Her fastidious father inched away from her. After two days and nights, the little band arrived in Chicago. Basha, without much dignity, self-respect, or grace, rushed wailing into her sister's arms. They cried and laughed at the same time, children underfoot and miserable, bewildered. Beril and the sister's husband, Abe, looked on with embarrassment.

The sister's apartment was a mess, a hovel, which made the house in Rome a palace by comparison, though Basha's sister, Esther Fenstermacher, was happily unaware of the disarray she and hers abided in: a household consisting of the husband, an unemployed glazier, and twelve snotty-nosed children—they should live and be well—all untended, unwashed, unkempt, except for the oldest, one in the advanced stages of tuberculosis. Abandoning all hopes of a synagogue of his own for the present, Beril set out to find a job. Esther was no help. She was too happily engaged in her other good works, collecting money for every Jewish social work society, agency, and organization imaginable, determined to feed all starving Jewish families the world over, but her own. Beril and Basha, unable to stay with the Fenstermacher crew, found a small dark railroad flat under the rattling shadow of the Loop.

One day, after weeks and weeks of looking for work, he found himself staring at two recruiting posters: one of a well-fed doughboy with rosy cheeks, the other of an Uncle Sam with even rosier cheeks, pointing directly at him. UNCLE SAM WANTS YOU! Me? The solution to everything came to him, drastic though it was. He would enlist. The recruiting sergeant, patient and kind with this young greenhorn, brought up the matter of Beril's family.

"That's why I'm here," Beril explained. He amended the statement with a smile. That is, he was there as a man, as a father, but he owed something to his country too, no? He wished to do his duty. And in what capacity did he wish to serve? the sergeant asked gravely, writing it all down. As a chaplain. He was a man of the cloth, Beril pointed out, in more general terms, an ordained minister. Ah, but the ranks of the chaplains, it seemed—shuffling of papers—were, er, closed. Perhaps soon there would be more openings. With the war going on as it was . . . Beril nodded respectfully, courteously, as between men. He had naturally not taken off his hat during the interview, but now he made the gesture of tipping it. On the street, Beril thought again of becoming a pioneer in Palestine, of joining a troupe of traveling actors, but that would not solve the problem of a hungry family. Basha was overjoyed by his being rejected, but tried to hide her true feelings. Only jolly Esther took it upon herself to laugh at young Beril being a chaplain in the U.S. Army. For her it was like serving under the czar, different conditions notwithstanding. The search for a job continued.

No jobs? Impossible. Possible. My father couldn't quite credit this. Chicago, a wartime town, was bustling if not booming. But so far all he had been offered was a chance to sell toilet deodorants on commission. Since the idea of selling had been introduced, Esther's husband, Abe, had a brainstorm of his own. Why not sell insurance? "You have a million-dollar personality," Abe said. "I do?" Beril said, unable to think in such sums, and not exactly knowing what insurance was. Nevertheless, after Abe explained the principle of the thing to him, he agreed that it was a good idea. After all, personality aside, hadn't he almost succeeded in becoming a chaplain—which equaled officer—in the United States Army? That he had in fact failed escaped everyone for the moment. And it wasn't exactly selling, but more a matter of printed papers, clauses, signatures on dotted lines. He got some blank policies from Prudential of Illinois and made his first few calls, on Esther's fellow society members. Charming occasions, during which Beril exuded wit and wisdom, and got the idea that not only his own wife considered his mustache handsome. There was much tea served and accepted, strudel consumed. His potential customers were more and more taken with him. The only problem being that they remained potential. One day he almost succeeded in selling a policy to himself and finally came to his senses. The idea of insurance per se still intrigued him—it was certainly better than this other American custom of making a will—but what next? He stared out of the Fenstermacher window at a bleak winter sky. He was twenty-six years old. Esther's sickest child was coughing blood and phlegm into a basin.

Gradually he became aware that at the dining-room table, someone was gazing at him with large liquid eyes. It was Lily Fenstermacher, Esther's lovely sixteen-year-old daughter, who had been sitting, pen poised, over a diary with a gold clasp. As Beril returned her gaze, she trembled violently, then snapped the clasp shut, stowing away the diary in the one drawer allotted to her, in the china closet, though it seemed to be full of underwear. Then she went quickly to tend to her sick little brother on the couch, smoothing his forehead with cool damp cloths wrung out, feeding him chicken soup with a spoon. Esther, sailing in from one of her societies, refused to believe it when Lily said the child was getting worse. There were sicker children in foreign lands. She had sketches and photographs to prove it. Even when a doctor was finally called in, a professor in a frock coat and pince-nez dangling from a cord, and confirmed the gravity of the situation, she remained adamant in her optimism. The doctor did not stay long. He had even sicker patients to attend to. There was a new pestilence abroad in this land. Practically every house was struck with it. Schools and public buildings were closed. The papers were full of it. A plague, almost. Influenza.

One day, Beril came home from not selling insurance to find Basha sunk in a chair, unable to move. Her once wan cheeks were red and feverish. Her dark eyes glittered with panic. Beril took one look, inserted a thermometer into her rectally, overriding her anguished modesty, read 105, and hustled her into a flannel nightgown, then covered her with the big down comforter that had been part of her Russian dowry. He gave her tea with lemon and a lump of sugar to suck between her teeth, and when she had sipped at it slowly, obediently, like a grateful child, dressed his three actual children and brought them over to their Aunt Esther. He didn't want to leave them there in that mess, and there was also the matter of the consumptive child, but what choice was there? *"None, Beril, none!"* Lily cried, gazing at him with stricken eyes. She gathered the children to her passionately. "I swear to you I'll take care of them as if they were my own . . . that is . . . I mean, I never really meant her to . . . *Oy, gotenyu!*" Abandoning the children for a moment, she searched out the gilt-clasped diary and threw it down the dumbwaiter as if she and it had plunged into some fiery abyss. Beril and the children looked at her, mystified. When she had recovered, Beril went home.

Each day Basha's temperature fluctuated. Sometimes

she was clear-eyed and wanly cheerful, sometimes on the verge of delirium. Each evening Beril came over to Esther's, embraced his children, accepted the gift of a kugel wrapped in a napkin or a jar of soup from Lily, and hurried back. The frock-coated professor, when called in, shook his head. One morning at five, Basha's soft moans awakened her dozing husband. He stumbled from his bed to hers. Tears trickled down his face into his mustache, and he averted his gaze to the cold dawn so as not to frighten her. But she was almost beyond recognizing him. He stroked her thin wasted hand, stroked the wedding ring, the ring with the green stone, and then she gave him one of her gentlest smiles and died. Just died. "Blessed is the righteous judge," Beril murmured, and smoothed her disheveled hair, closed her eyelids with his fingertips, pulled the comforter over her face. He remembered them in steerage, and the joy and excitement of the arrival in this strange new world. The *goldene medina*. The half house. But he could not give himself over to grief, not just yet. There were his children, always and perpetually his children, down to and including Malke Leah. When he had finished davening, he called in a neighbor to watch over Basha's body and hastened to Esther's apartment, where he was met with loud weeping and wailing. Esther hugged and squeezed the children, calling them orphans and frightening them out of their wits. Beril was annoyed, he had meant to tell them quietly and gently, quote a parable or two, with perhaps Lily watching and learning on the side, leaning on one elbow. But why was he thinking of Lily at such a moment?

After the funeral, a bereaved Beril sat shiva at Esther's house. Seven days of bedlam, the house full of relatives, *landslayt*, Esther's society members. More weeping and wailing, also laughter, sweets, covered baked dishes, tey-glach, pastries without number. His own children stood always in corners in a cluster of three, in size places, Samuel Joseph, Sarah Rachel, and Malke Leah, who occasionally sat down with a thump. Some idiot of a relative would then announce to them anew that they were orphans, and the children would cry loudly and cling to each other, not to him. Otherwise they stood in dark-eyed silence until someone, usually Lily, remembered to feed them, clothe them, wash them, pull up their sagging black stockings, give them an album with pictures. How had Lily, for the most part, managed to remain sane and sweet in this madhouse? The windows and mirrors, anything that could reflect a face or form, were soaped over. The relatives sat on hard wooden benches in their stockinged feet. The lapel of Beril's only jacket was slashed, the mark of the mourner. A yahrzeit candle burned on the sideboard amid Esther's scrolls and *pushkes*. Kaddish four times a day. There were always plenty of people to make a minyan.

Then it was finally over. Beril, as rabbi, escorted the mourners around the block, children included, and marched them all upstairs again where they ate hard-boiled eggs and bagels—circles, endless circles to suggest infinity—pronounced a few *brochas*, and fell silent. What to do now? Life in whatever shape still waited. Beril called his children to him, formally. Lily ushered the three over, shooing away one or two extras. Beril looked down at them benignly. "Children," he began, "fear not the sentence of death, for it is the sentence that the Lord . . ." This was too deep for them. They stared up at him, then at one another, clearly on the verge of caterwauling. "Death," Beril recommenced hastily—Lily nodded encouragement—"death is not always an end, *kinder*, it is also a beginning." So far so good. Now, how to proceed from here? Lily nodded again. If only she would stop nodding. Never mind. "Remember that always, *kinder*," Beril concluded, not sure how he had arrived at his destination. "Death is a beginning as well as an end."

He bundled them up and, despite Esther's protests, took them home. They all stood around aimlessly. Beril went downstairs, purchased a few carrots, some soup greens, a chicken, paid the woman to pluck the fowl, and carried it all back upstairs. With an air of authority, he filled a pot with boiling water, plunged the chicken in, after a suitable interval took it out, and served it up on soup plates. The children took one taste and looked up at him. He had forgotten the salt and God knew what else. He regarded them as the stern patriarch he had now become. The children dug in hurriedly and finally ate like normal folk. "It's good, *tateh*," Malke Leah, the monkey, finally announced, as if he needed her endorsement. "Good, good," the others chimed in. He nodded, satisfied that he was now established as the ultimate supreme authority of his ragged household.

None of Beril's brothers had come to the funeral, but only Cathrael apologized. He had too recently suffered a loss of his own, little golden-haired Hadassah—fifth on line after his own Shmuel Yosef, Anna, Meyer Isaac, Oscar Brandeis—victim of a hit-and-run driver. Fredel remained inconsolable, though it was against God's law to remain inconsolable. For himself at least he had his studies and his business, which was thriving. People wanted furniture these days, it seemed, and also fine fabrics, which Cathrael sold by the yard, though in his heart he

remained an artisan. Perhaps Beril would come to Norfolk
one day soon, bringing the children. There were many
newcomers to Norfolk, including fine Jewish families with
many fine sons and daughters. The thought of exposing
his children to Fredel's adder tongue, not to mention her
cooking, after they had just been through so much did not
appeal to Beril. There was also another underlying theme
in Cathrael's letter that he chose to ignore for the moment. He thanked Cathrael for writing and they both assured each other they would write again soon.

While Beril was dismissing Norfolk, at least temporar-
ily—he had had enough of the South—one of Beril's potential "customers" had come up with an idea. A realtor
of sorts, he had first considered enlisting Beril's help in
selling real estate, but with my father's track record in
insurance . . . In any case, there was no point in going
back when forward was better. Why, then, shouldn't Beril
become a fund raiser, specifically for a new tuberculosis
sanitarium in Denver? The idea of tuberculosis as such
was not too appealing—he had seen too much of it at close
hand in Esther's house. But fund raising was another matter. Beril knew himself to be a persuasive orator, given
the chance, and then there was an honored tradition in
Europe of rabbis traveling about to raise money for their
yeshivas. The matter was discussed with Esther, Abe, and
as a silent partner, Lily. All agreed that it was an excellent
notion, including a downcast Lily, who seemed about to
erupt into speech but merely kept nodding.

Beril met with the sanitarium's representative in Chicago, at a kosher restaurant. It was a successful meeting.
Terms were discussed, and also traveling arrangements,
which considering that my father was a young widower on
his own would not be too difficult. A handshake over tea

and compote and Beril accepted what was no longer a job but a position. Speeches were already running through his head. He left Esther to go through her sister's few possessions, keeping for himself only a few photos which he did not look at, and the eyeglasses, and also the dark gold wedding ring and the ring with the green stone. Esther would also decide to which charity she would give the few sticks of furniture. He brought the children over to Esther's apartment for one last time. More weeping, wailing, pants wetting, refusals to eat—how many times must this scene be enacted? Then he had only to pack his own small valise and be off. But first a trip to the cemetery to visit Basha's newly frozen, snowy grave. Lily went with him. Beril, still without an overcoat, turned up the slashed collar of his jacket, and looked down at the grave, trying to remember Basha as she was when alive, and unable to. He knew she would come to him in his dreams. "Beril?" Lily murmured, almost but not quite reaching out a hand to him. He turned his good ear. Her eyelashes were wet with tears and snow. Her lips trembled as if something were welling up in her heart. Then Lily shook her head and smiled, and together they left the cemetery.

The road was not as fine an arena for his talents as Beril had expected, but it was certainly finer than any he had known before. He gave many speeches in drafty halls and synagogue basements. Sometimes he was treated as a mendicant, eating herring in dingy restaurants, sleeping in shabby rooms in Jewish boarding houses. Sometimes he arrived as a noted orator with posters advertising him in advance, and addressed a crowded hall. No matter how large or small the audience, he spoke with passion, in honor of the sanitarium's location in Denver, throwing in references to forty years in the desert, and ending with a fervent plea for funds. They were to give until it hurt, an idea that did not always appeal to them. Nevertheless, the women wept—entertained by any idea of suffering—the men applauded.

Occasionally at a soiree afterward, given by one of the local balabatim, Beril encountered a kind of woman he had never met before. Cigarette smokers in Russian blouses and with arms akimbo, they looked at him with mocking smiles and were almost always called Tanya or Masha. Unmarried. For some reason they reminded him of Lily back in Chicago, though she didn't actually resemble them in the least. From here his mind went on to Cathrael in Virginia, who was writing more and more of the fine Jewish families in Norfolk, with increasing emphasis on the daughters instead of the sons. And indeed what was a man without a wife and home? Beril answered noncommittally, knowing that he would have to face this music sooner or later, but putting it off.

For the first time in his life he was enjoying himself. He was becoming a seasoned traveler, seedy rooming houses or not. He ate in kosher restaurants, graduating from herring to the full menu, was entertained increasingly in fine homes, practically a guest of honor, the sultry Russian girls smiling at him seductively from their corners. He was not only an orator, but a cuff-shooter, well-dressed and dapper. His eyeglasses had black rims to them. He had bought an overcoat at last, a gray chesterfield with a black velvet collar, plus a black felt hat, and a cane with an amber top. He went to the theater, reacquainting himself with *Shulamith* and other Goldfadn plays, seeing Jacob Adler for the first time, and Boris Thomashevsky, and Ludwig

Satz. His letters to Chicago were rich with triumph, to be read avidly by Esther and her society mates. What she did with the enclosed money orders was another matter. But Abe was unemployed and Lily was being courted by a beginning accountant. Lily herself did not mention the man, and only painted glorious pictures of the children. When her consumptive brother died, Beril whipped in and out for the funeral, traveling all night sitting up, though he did not say so, not even to Lily, who guessed. His glowing children were not so glowing. In fact, even though they had been hastily washed and dressed, they looked like tattered little Fenstermachers. But this was not a suitable time to express his displeasure. On the next trip he would bring them bigger, better presents. The children's eyes widened anyhow, as if they couldn't believe he had ever belonged to them, this handsome young Papa.

Beril continued to send them gifts and clothes from the road, and also tried to set aside enough money to get his twin sisters married. His next speaking engagement took him to Evanston, which was near enough to Chicago to make a side trip worthwhile. He decided to pay his family a surprise visit, with first a stop at Marshall Field. Once, in their cold huddled wanderings, he and Lily had found themselves in Marshall Field, more to get warm than to gape. But gape they did. Such counters, merchandise, chandeliers. The other shoppers had glanced at them with distaste, as did the floorwalker, who asked them in a high-pitched nasal voice what it was they wanted. Lily had been too dazzled to notice that anything was wrong, but Beril did. He had hustled Lily out, determined that when and if he ever visited that store again, he would come as a gentleman.

Today, his dream had come true. He pushed through the revolving doors in triumph, such triumph that he found himself out on the street and had to do it all over again, finally and successfully depositing himself inside the store. The floorwalker, obsequious and with carnation, wringing his hands, asked if he could be of any assistance. Indeed. Beril wished to be directed to the children's department. He ascended in a grilled elevator and entered a wonderland. A salesgirl, seeing him wandering about with an armful of stuffed animals, a pup, a kitty cat, a teddy bear, all of the finest velour and plush, tried to help him. He described the sizes of his children with charming ineptitude, impossible gestures, and ultimately ordered outfits for all of them, a tweed knickered suit for Samuel Joseph, two identical pale blue coats for his daughters, which came with matching bonnets and leggings. The coats had little brown mouton collars, which had the look of genuine beaver. He could see their plump little chins nestled into them, though wall-eyed Sarah Rachel in particular was neither plump nor rosy, but on the skinny side, like her mother. He paid in cash, doling out the bills grandly. Laden with gift-wrapped packages, he descended and emerged, hailing a taxi with his amber-topped cane. As he made his grand entrance into Esther's apartment, however, all hell broke loose. Children scampered away like field mice. Abe arose and immediately absented himself from this unexpected felicity. Only Lily remained, dumbfounded. She had been lolling on the couch in a Chinese kimono, one leg extended, pulling on a red silk stocking, clearly getting ready for a date with her accountant. What appeared to be another gilt-clasped diary was open at her side. She dropped the leg, and hastily pulled the kimono around her. *"Beril,"* she whispered huskily.

Too late. Beril turned away, glaring, and deposited his gift-wrapped packages on the table. His eye lit on the corner, where his three lost lambs stood in their usual posture of abject terror. Did they not see that this was their father, their Moses come to rescue them? His tired, huddled masses yearning to be free. Sighing impatiently, Beril beckoned them over. Like little ravenous beasts, they proceeded to tear open the wrong packages. He sorted them out, and set them at it again. They were curiously disappointed. Evidently, by now clothes had no meaning for them at all, much less finery. Never mind. Ignoring Lily's pleas to help, he tried their new outfits on them one by one, starting with Samuel Joseph's knickers, noting a pair of sleeves to be shortened here, a hem there. Esther emerged from wherever it was she had been hiding. He had bought her a tortoiseshell comb for her hair, for Abe a tortoiseshell cigar holder, for Lily a string of amber beads, over which she burst into tears. Esther and Abe regarded him defensively. "Thank you, Beril," Lily sobbed. "Thank you, *tateh*," the children chorused, led off by the littlest. It was a mess. He took the first train back to Evanston, not wishing to stay any longer in the Fenstermacher pesthole than he had to, but knowing he would soon have to return. And not alone. (He thought of his bedraggled three in their oversize finery, of Lily in her open kimono pulling on red stockings for her accountant.) But with a wife.

More letters back and forth, more money orders absconded, more misleading rosy communiqués from Lily, that woman of easy virtue, that *nafke*. At first Beril considered the possibility of continuing his travels and leaving whoever it was alone with the children. But reason took over. That such a woman did not exist, he already knew. Sighing, he wrote a letter to Cathrael inviting himself down, and on a hunch, to Yankel's rabbi in Brooklyn. The rabbi did not immediately answer, but Cathrael was overjoyed.

It was wonderful to see this older brother after all these years. Cathrael was still handsome and swarthy, still smiling. At the station they kissed on the lips. The same with Fredel at home, who smelled of onions and herring. How Cathrael abided her, Beril did not understand. But hadn't the rabbi of Vitebsk in a similar situation said, "If I had not married her, who else would?" The children, considering half their parentage, had turned out not too badly, the older girl, Anna, a bit horse-faced, Samuel Joseph a bit simple, Oscar Brandeis a bit glum, the middle son, Meyer Isaac, the only one who took after his father in wit and charm. Little dead Hadassah's picture stood in a silver frame on the Jamestown chest. The story of her early and tragic demise was told and retold, before Fredel's dinner and after Fredel's dinner, no details omitted, including the make of the car. In the midst of his chess game, Beril brushed away a genuine tear.

The next morning in the synagogue, still suffering from indigestion, Beril was introduced to Rabbi Gordon, and then to one Moses Gordon, no relation, a pious sot, with round red cheeks and a gray goatee. To turn from the rabbi, an old friend of both Lekhem's and Finkel's, to the other man, clearly Fredel's connection, took some doing, but Beril did it. He and Cathrael were invited to partake of a little glass of tea at the Gordon abode that very afternoon. In a spirit of fatalism, Beril accepted for himself and his brother. The abode turned out to be in the poorest section of town, above the family's ramshackle grocery store, redolent of its goods and its customers, mostly indigent Negroes. There were tobacco, flour, potatoes, candy, crackers, plus a giant clove-studded brown ham on the counter. Beril averted his eyes as he followed the men up the wooden steps that led to the living quarters. He had never seen a ham at such close range before, much less a brown one.

He and Cathrael were invited to sit down at a formally set table, complete with steaming brass samovar, best silver, glasses, and saucers. There were plates of strudel, teyglach, honey cake, sponge cake, slices of lemon, various preserves, all the doing of Moses' eldest daughter, Clara, who was evidently a great housekeeper, a true *berye*. So far so good. Eventually, after a suitable interval when everything else under the sun had been discussed, Clara entered shyly to see if she could get them anything more. What else was there to get? She retreated, a little clumsily. But not before her eyes and Beril's had met. Hers were green, her hair honey blond. She was wearing a plump black lace shirtwaist blouse, a black sateen hobble skirt, and a cameo brooch. After another suitable interval, Beril consulted his wristwatch. From his vest pocket Moses withdrew a large gold timepiece studded with a diamond chip. The two brothers had hardly eaten enough to do Clara justice, but it was time to be off. As they emerged from the store, Beril looked back. Clara was peering at him through a part in the window curtains. "Come back from there, *klutz!*" he heard Moses Gordon say. Beril sighed. Back on the road, Beril sent more letters and money orders to Chicago, this time asking the children delicately what they would think of having a new mother. Little Yosel marveled at this message, inquiring in his childish scrawl how there could be a new mother when they didn't have an old one. On perfumed stationery, Lily hinted that in this country engagements could be broken. Beril ignored her.

Another visit to Norfolk. This time Beril meant business. A prolonged courtship was no good for anyone, and besides, Yankel's rabbi had sent word that there was an opening for a rabbi in a new congregation in Canarsie. Where this was, Beril had no idea, somewhere in the outer reaches of Brooklyn, but he accepted at once, sending along his *smicha* and a letter from Rabbi Gordon and one from Rabbi Lekhem, the latter so deep in scholarship as to be almost incomprehensible. Encouraged by the job development, he called on Clara again, this time alone, flowers in hand, shooting his cuffs, handing over his amber-handled cane, which she took from him with some bewilderment. She put it finally on the floor, alongside a torn umbrella. They sat down stiffly and tried to talk. They had nothing to say to each other. So far so good. She was built for motherhood—to more than his three?—modest enough not to want to thrust herself into his limelight. He took his leave, and then returned for another evening of nonconversation, first running the gauntlet of old Moses with his spurious Talmudic quotations—Beril suffered in silence—and also Clara's smirking brother, Alex, who had the habit, possibly congenital, of chewing toothpicks as he surveyed the scene.

Another night, he took Clara to the theater, a production of *The Dybbuk*, which was so deep, the Yiddish so high-flown, that she couldn't understand a word. He had bought her a two-pound box of chocolates with a white satin ribbon beforehand, and this she munched on warily during intermission. Beril told her of his travels, of other plays he had seen, the interesting people he had met, and rendered Clara totally speechless. *Nu.* What could you do? Beril was satisfied. Cathrael was satisfied. Fredel was Fredel. Clara had had other suitors, among them a rich carpenter, but she had always wanted a man with education, and this Beril certainly had, plus the *yiches* of being a rabbi. The only fly in her ointment was that she desperately missed her mother, and the other sisters and brothers who were still in the Ukrainian province of Podolya. A wedding date was set for the end of November. Rabbi Gordon was to perform the ceremony, which would take place in the synagogue with a reception afterward that would feature Fredel's cooking. It was again not quite the fate that Beril had in mind for himself. But again, *nu.* He had found a mother for his children, his first duty. A *berye.* What Clara would make of the poor little wretches he shuddered to think. Maybe after she had cleaned them up . . . ? He had a sudden intimation that maybe Clara would be a little bit too much of a *berye.*

The wedding took place as planned, Beril in a brown suit and a small black yarmulke, Clara in a beige lace shirt-waist and an impossible hat. Rabbi Lekhem sent one of his sons as ambassador, and the son was introduced to Cathrael's daughter, Anna, not casually. Seven times around the altar, the whole lot of them. Beril stepped on the glass. A quick kiss. Cries of *"Mazel tov!"* All went off to Cathrael's house, having steeled themselves beforehand with sedlitz powders against the well-known exigencies of Fredel's cuisine. Tears, laughter, jokes (Clara's brother had to be reminded with a nudge of Rabbi Gordon's presence), merrymaking, enormous quantities of indigestible food, wine, schnapps, a plenitude of *brochas,* a song by Alex about his *shtetele* Belz, a town that he had never laid eyes on. Finally a speech by Moses, exhorting the blessings of God upon the happy pair and admonishing his son-in-law to take care of the precious jewel, meaning Clara, that he was entrusting to him. Beril laid a light hand on his mouth, reminded of his sensitive stomach. People were departing. It was time for him and Clara to leave too, though Beril was not in much of a hurry. It was really not such a bad party, after all, and even Fredel was beginning to look good to him. But Meyer Isaac was waiting outside in Cathrael's car. He suddenly wished his mother were there. Clara wished *her* mother were there. Thus united, the happy pair embarked on their first and last honeymoon, Meyer Isaac at the wheel.

Their destination was a farm not far off in the Virginia countryside. It was the best my father had been able to come up with since a place like Florida—he still thought of Florida—was out of the question. Meyer Isaac helped them out with their bags, assisted by the farmer, a Jewish farmer, and then when everything had been safely carried upstairs, Beril and Clara sat themselves on the lumpy bed, and looked down at the floral carpet. He wondered why she had not sought the modest comfort of their only chair, but there was already a side to this girl that had not been evident in Basha. A cowbell. Suppertime was approaching. Beril said a few *brochas,* washed up in water from an ice cold jug, also floral-patterned. Everything in the room was floral-patterned except for the bedspread, which was white tufted chenille. He felt he was seeing it all too vividly. Clara removed her hat, jabbing it with a hatpin, and they descended. Neither of them had unpacked yet. They sat down at the table with the farmer and his wife, an old gnarled pair. Both were a little deaf, and since Beril had his bad ear to contend with, and Clara never said much anyway (would she make up for it later?), there was little by way of urbane dinner conversation. There was plenty to eat, however: goose, which left greasy deposits around Clara's mouth and on the farmer's red flannel undershirt, vast amounts of vegetables, cabbage, carrots, spinach, pickled cucumbers, potatoes, kasha, tea, compote, cakes.

Stuffed, Beril pushed back his chair and suggested a stroll. He raced upstairs to retrieve their wraps, took a look at the bed, raced down again. They opened the screen door to the porch and took deep breaths of the fresh night air. Beril raised his head to look up at the stars and realized his nose was running. The ground was pocked and icy. They walked slowly around the frozen yard. Clara slipped suddenly and Beril put out his hand to steady her. The touch had an unpredictable effect on him and he thought more kindly of the lumpy bed. Presently, having uttered no more than two or three words to each other, they turned and went inside. Beril told Clara to go upstairs first and she went. From the parlor, he heard her stomping around overhead, ominous sounds, then a vast creak, then silence. The farmer and his wife had turned in also, which was too bad. He would have liked to chat a bit, make up for the postprandial silence, offer one of his Turkish cigarettes from the sporty tin box, a habit recently acquired. However. He rose, flipped his cigarette under the lid of the black iron stove, replaced it with a clang, then mounted the stairs. Gentlemanly, he knocked first and peered in afterward. Clara was safely in bed and all unpacked. He decided to save his own unpacking for the next day and rummaged around in his valise until he found a pair of flannel pajamas and a toothbrush. He sauntered off to the cold bathroom with a towel slung over his arm. Returning a few minutes later, mouth a bit toothpasty, he repeated the knocking and the peering. In the light of the hurricane lamp by the bedside, Clara seemed asleep, honey plait down one shoulder. He climbed into bed beside her, covering himself to the chin with a coarse blanket, half-asleep himself. . . . However . . . He poked her in the shoulder. "Clara?" "Hm . . . ?" "It's Beril." "I know." So far so good. He turned over and before he had a chance to take her in his arms, she had obediently raised her nightgown to breast level. Decidedly, this was no Basha! But the breasts were large and warm and cushiony. Still struggling with sleep, he overcame it.

Morning. A farmyard morning. Bright, crisp, cold, clear, sunny. Air redolent of pine needles and the barnyard. Once more they strolled, now arm in arm. Beril was wearing a black fruitman's sweater and freezing to death. But he had pictured it as proper country attire. Clara was in her beige coat and the unfortunate hat, curved mid-height heels. By now he couldn't imagine her in any other outdoor outfit, she was so impervious to change, to any normal wear and tear. But in bed another matter, that he preferred not to dwell on now, nor of the amazing things he had murmured in her ear, nor of the more amazing things that had gone through his mind. Afterward, Clara had calmly climbed out of bed, inspected the sheets by the light of the hurricane lamp, pointed out the bloodstains, knotted them up, and given them to him. "What am I supposed to do with these?" Beril had demanded.

"Show them to Fredel," Clara had said, replacing them with another set she had thoughtfully brought along with her. The pillowcases she left unchanged.

But now the hot blood of the night was passed, real or otherwise, and here they were picking their way carefully amid the gravel. Cows mooed, chickens squawked. They took a carriage ride. Clip, clop, clip, clop, they might have been in Russia. Only, the farmer's wife was driving. Well, nothing in life was quite what one expected, was it? Beril put his arm expansively around Clara's plump shoulders, knocking her hat somewhat askew. She primly adjusted it, making clear what her priorities were. Then lunch, all *milchik* and very healthy—Beril felt he had already gained ten pounds—and up to nap. They slept miles apart—sex was not for the afternoon—and woke shaking themselves like geese. Clara descended first. She was a bit bolder today. Then another sashay around the farmyard. The beasts were in their stalls, including the bull, thank God. When they entered the house again, Beril went into the parlor, Clara into the kitchen, where she helped the farm wife slice cabbage, exchanging a little woman talk, recipes. Then dinner, and again to bed.

The next day the same, and the next, and the next. By the end of the week, Beril was exhausted. He could not face much more of this, though he had contracted for two weeks. Besides, there were the abandoned children to think of, the house in Canarsie that the new congregation had found and expected him to move into. Without telling Clara, he rode into town one afternoon with the farmer while she was napping, and whipped off a telegram to Lily in Chicago: HOW ARE THE CHILDREN STOP SEND WORD IMMEDIATELY STOP BEST WISHES STOP SIGNED BERIL. Lily fired back a wire. THE CHILDREN ARE AS WELL AS

CAN BE EXPECTED STOP MANY GREETINGS STOP SIGNED LILY (FENSTERMACHER). Beril was decided. He and Clara would return at once to Norfolk, and from there he would go to Chicago, leaving her safely in the bosom of her family for a few days. They would all rendezvous in New York, Clara going on ahead to prepare the house, accompanied by her brother Alex who had always wanted to travel anyway. A complicated plan. Clara was so distraught and bewildered, he feared she would remain in that state the rest of her life. Leaving her with her father like a piece of merchandise on deposit, Beril gave her and Alex two sleeper tickets and set forth for Chicago.

The children were in worse shape than ever—what a life he foresaw for himself!—Lily red-eyed and weeping. He gave her short shrift, though he allowed her to help him get the children more or less ready for their journey. As usual, half the Marshall Field stuff had disappeared, but he had too much on his hands to worry about such matters now. He said good-bye curtly to Esther and unemployed Abe, left a few dollars for the charities, and permitted Lily to accompany him to the station. The children, who had never been told exactly where they were going and who now seemed to believe *Lily* was their mother, started to wail. Amid this cacophony, the train departed. Beril did not see Lily weeping and waving on the platform until they had almost chugged from sight. She was certainly deeply attached to the children, and also, curiously, to a string of amber beads which she kept pointing to. No matter. The journey was already a nightmare, the stuff of family legends, if anybody should survive it. At great expense he had purchased two sleepers for the four of them, couching man and boy together in the upper berth, the two girls in the lower, exhorted

Sarah to be a little *mameleh* and mind Malke Leah, but all night long the corridor resounded with the combined cries of "Papa-Lily!" "Pee-pee, pee-pee!" and all the rest of it, so that the Pullman porter, who had started out telling them with a grin that his name was George, muttered increasingly about retiring.

In the morning, having put them together as well as he could, released Malke Leah from the bathroom where she had locked herself in, escorted them in and out of the diner, Beril was a wreck. He wished he had not told Clara and brother to meet them at the station. Malke Leah, needless to say, had puked all over him, wet her pants. Sarah Rachel had lost her new doll. She insisted she had left it in the diner, where it wasn't. Then Malke Leah, not to be outdone, threw the Masonic ring Beril had given her to play with (good-bye, Cherokee Lodge) out the window, which shouldn't have been opened in December in the first place, except that Samuel Joseph on whom Beril thought he could depend, his little man as he had called him, was carsick. Some little man. Never mind. He buttoned them up crookedly, pulled up leggings, pulled down coats, tied bonnets, wiped noses, and they descended into a long black tunnel—a portent of things to come? All atumble, they alit.

And there they were. Clara and her toothpick-chewing brother, Beril and his brood. He had of course not mentioned Clara's existence, and so now merely said brightly, "This is your new mother." What new mother? They all glanced around for a dimly remembered other life, then let out a howl. A little island of turmoil in Grand Central Station. Clara looked at them and then at Beril with green eyes turned beady. Alex glumly shifted his toothpick from one side of his mouth to the other. Only little Yosel was smitten and looked at Clara as if he were seeing a blond angel.

Destination: Canarsie, Brooklyn. They rode out in two taxis, Clara in one with her brother, Beril in the other with the three children, who had refused to let him out of their sight, again a grim portent of things to come. Could one reverse the clock in such matters? Why had he married? Why not a full-time housekeeper, modern style, for the children, and for himself a Russianized beauty with cigarette smoke curling up toward her gleaming eyes? Too late. They had already arrived at the house, which wasn't half bad, now that Beril considered it from all directions. The children looked at each other with their usual fear and trembling, evidently not having yet grasped that not only had they acquired a new mother but a new home. Beril cleared his throat, about to launch on a short, pithy peroration. *"Kinder,"* he commenced. But Clara, who had arrived first and looked as if she had put on her apron before she had finished taking off her coat, was already shooing them inside, straight up to the bathroom, Samuel Joseph in the lead, Malke Leah hanging on to Sarah Rachel's coattails.

"Maybe they're hungry?" Beril suggested over the rushing water of the tub. "They're *shmutzik,"* Clara said. Beril took one last look at his crew, and sauntered out nonchalantly. On the way down, he offered Alex a Turkish cigarette, which Alex put behind his ear. He thought of the first house he and Basha had rented, a half house really, so what did he know about houses? This one looked very clean at least, though Clara said it had been very *shmutzik*, and the children would be cleaner, to judge from the yowls of protest.

In a while they descended, outraged, violated, red and raw from scrubbing. Taking off a damp apron and putting on a dry one, Clara marched into the kitchen, expecting and asking aid from no one. Soon pleasing aromas wafted through the air. Suffering pangs of hunger, Beril and his three waited until they were invited into the kitchen, where Clara, the *berye*, had already laid out chicken and tsimmes, potato kugel, sliced cucumbers and onions with vinegar. For Alex, whom cucumbers gave gas, a single portion of beets. Clara served from behind, doing the dishes while they were still eating, banging away at pots and pans. After lunch came laundry—but so *much* of it? Beril wondered, asking himself where he and Lily had gone wrong. On top of the stove, where tasty morsels had once simmered, there was now a black cauldron into which Clara had plunged everything she could lay her hands on, including things from Marshall Field that ought to have been sent to the French dry cleaner. In the sink stood a washboard, half-covered with suds. When everything had been boiled, scrubbed, beaten with a brush, rinsed and wrung, Clara went out to the yard to hang her wash in the crisp cold December air. Beril took a short turn around the block. When he came back, it was all stiff as boards.

After the laundry, dinner. A light repast of blintzes, cottage cheese, sour cream, chopped up raw vegetables, tea, preserves. By now the children were too limp to eat anything, and went up to bed immediately, as instructed. Then Alex. Beril and Clara followed, putting out the lights. In the bedroom, Clara undid her corset, scratching where it had dug into her ribs. She climbed into bed, with Beril in his flannel honeymoon pajamas following suit. Clara yawned. Could it all possibly wait until tomorrow? But no. Clara lay there with an air of placid expectancy. It was the first time she had been placid all day, so perhaps it would be best to take advantage of it. He raised his eyebrows questioningly, Clara rolled over toward him.

But wait. Beril had heard something. "Clara, did you hear something?" "No." But it was a sound that could not be ignored, like the bleat of two piteous calves. With a murmur of apology, Beril got out of bed and padded in bare feet to the bedroom next door. Where one little girl should have been neatly tucked into each cot, there were now two huddled together, their kinky hair entangled on the same pillow. Sarah Rachel held Malke Leah in her arms. "What is it?" Beril said. "She had a dream," Sarah Rachel whispered. "She dreamed a big blond witch was coming to eat her up." Some dream. "Dreams can't hurt you," Beril said. "They can, they can!" Malke cried. "*Shah*," Beril said, "*shah*." He carried Malke Leah back to her own bed, felt her forehead to make sure it wasn't hot, felt Sarah Rachel's feet to make sure they weren't cold, and tiptoed out. The floor was icy—he must buy a runner for this hall—and by the time he reached Clara the sound had started again. They both stiffened, and tried to wait it out. It was no use. Murmuring another apology, Beril repeated his trek next door, again removing Malke Leah from Sarah Rachel's bed. "Don't be a baby," Beril said, covering her to the chin. "You don't want to be a baby, do you?" "No, *tateh*." "Tomorrow I'll buy you a treat." "What kind?" "I don't know yet—Soreleh, make sure she doesn't get up again." In answer, Sarah Rachel's eye slid helplessly down into its accustomed corner. Again

{ 62 }

the plunge back into his bed. Clara heaved up and down like a hulk in a seastorm. This time he didn't reach out, but waited stiffly for what he knew was to come. "*Gey shoyn*," Clara said when it did, "go already." "Listen, Clara, I—" "Go." Dragging his pillow and extra blanket, Beril slept the rest of the night in Malke's cot.

By comparison with his home, the shul, within walking distance on account of shabbos, was an oasis. Ever since that first night, Clara had been giving him black looks, walking around with her mouth pursed. When she did speak, which happened with increasing frequency, it was of two-pound boxes of candy which had never fooled her, that as she had been a slave to her father . . . She never seemed to be out of her apron. The two girls now helped her with the dishes, Malke Leah on a step stool. Yosele brought her coal in a wagon, happy to do it. Alex, who had decided to settle down with them and look for a job, never got off his *tuchas*. But the shul, that was another matter. In the shul, which had named itself the Hebrew Educational Alliance, he discovered that he held all the important positions at once: rabbi, cantor, Hebrew school teacher. They had even given him an office, in which he hung his new rabbinical robes and two best talesim. That at morning services there were hardly enough people to make a minyan didn't bother him. That of those who did attend there were the usual yodelers and caterwaulers trying to outdo each other in prayer also didn't matter. That attendance at the Hebrew school was so low he immediately enrolled Samuel Joseph, Sarah Rachel, and as an afterthought, Malke Leah, was also of no consequence. That his salary was hardly a king's ransom made no difference. It was enough to support Clara and Alex and the children in the style to which they were becoming accustomed—though what he would do if Moses came up north to be a permanent boarder, as threatened, not to mention another brother and two sisters, who would soon be coming to America, he had no idea.

The important thing was that he loved his work, loved delivering his sermons on a Saturday morning, and shaking hands afterward. Yodelers notwithstanding, they were a modern up-to-date congregation, who enjoyed having a beardless young rabbi as much as he enjoyed them. Committees they formed at the drop of a hat, and there was even a Ladies Auxiliary of which the president's wife was president. "Do you want to join the Ladies Auxiliary, Clara?" "I'm not a society lady," Clara said bitterly, referring to Esther. Sometimes, locking up after their meetings, he found the president's wife in his office, licking stamps. And to cap it all, there was soon to be a testimonial dinner for the president himself, for which the wife was licking more and more stamps, and at which Beril had been invited to be principal speaker. The main problem was, should the speech be in Yiddish or English? The Saturday *droshes* were in Yiddish, and made the women cry. But for a state occasion, wouldn't English be better? The Hebrew would come at the end. *"Yivorechecha adonoy v'yishmorecha.* May the Lord bless you and keep you. *Yoer adonoy ponov elecha.* May the Lord cause his face to shine upon you. . . ." Hands upraised in benediction. He practiced in front of the bathroom mirror, while Alex waited none too patiently to get in—"They're showing movies in there?"—and Clara, who never laughed, laughed. He thought unwillingly of Lily, and how her eyes would shine out at him from the audience, and how she would converse with the president and other balabatim afterward, yet not make the women nervous. How at home there would be tea and learned conversations and even the chess cronies would be made to feel welcome. But Lily had married her accountant—did he take her shopping in Marshall Field? Back to the banquet.

"Maybe I shouldn't go," Clara said, as the day grew nearer.

"What do you mean you shouldn't go? You have to."

"Why?"

"Because you're my rebbetzin."

"And what about the children?"

"Alex will stay with them."

"I don't have a dress."

"So buy one."

"With what?"

"Money," Beril said, "money." And gave her some. She went out and bought a bargain, underscoring the point, though it was apparent. Blue chiffon, which barely made it over the armor of her corset. The blue satin shoes that she had had dyed to match hurt her feet before she had finished putting them on. The night of the banquet, Beril in tuxedo, wing collar, and chesterfield, helped her into her wedding coat and extended his arm. She nervously dusted her nose with a little more whitish Lady Esther face powder, and flattened the two dips on her forehead with a finger. They walked the few blocks to the synagogue. The long tables in the basement were adorned with ferns, ceiling and doorways festooned with crepe paper. Clara left her coat in the vestibule and timidly peered inside. For a moment, Beril's heart ached for her. Then it came time to make the introductions, since many members of the congregation had hardly laid eyes on her before. "My rebbetzin," Beril said with a touch of comic bravado he did not feel. One of the congregants, a young wise guy, asked if that meant their children would be rabbits. Beril gave a laugh, but at the word *children*, Clara's face hardened.

He escorted her quickly to the dais, a raised table at which the president and his wife and other important balabatim were already seated. The meal commenced with sweetbreads. After the consommé and the ubiquitous chicken, there was a general clearing of throats. One of the balabatim made a few "short" introductory remarks. The president's wife welcomed them all on behalf of the Ladies Auxiliary. Another one of the balabatim introduced the president, who went on for about an hour and a half. And now it was Beril's turn. He rose to the applause, shuffled through his papers, and laid them aside amid the ferns, having decided to speak extemporaneously. "Friends," he began, with a smile that was by now second nature to him, "honored guests, Mr. President, ladies and gentlemen. . . . The sages tell us . . ." From the first, he had their attention, except for Clara, who seemed to be dozing off. The jokes went well, and so did his serious points that they were leading up to. His English, he felt, was becoming more and more masterly. The tone was exactly right. He ended with the blessing, "And may the Lord cause His countenance to shine upon you and grant you everlasting peace," and sat down.

People leaned back and stretched a little, well satisfied. Only Clara remained with head bowed, an object of congratulation, though she looked the picture of dejection. The meal had obviously been hard for her, and even the familiar chicken had apparently looked unfamiliar to her.

For clues on silverware she had looked to either side of her. When the others lifted their drumsticks, she had followed suit, pinky upraised. Unfortunately she was left-handed, and whenever she used her knife to cut the stuffed kishke, she also jabbed the president in the ribs with her elbow. But now main course and speeches had been achieved, and ices and demitasses arrived.

"You have a charming husband," the president's wife said, applying herself to her dessert. "He doesn't even look like a rabbi."

"He doesn't look like a rabbi?" Clara's eyes narrowed.

"I mean he's so young, so handsome, so—"

"*Beril!*"

Beril stopped smiling.

"And you," the president added waggishly. "With that blond hair and those rosy cheeks, you look like a *Poylishe shikse.*"

"A *Poylishe shikse?*"

"Or, maybe you use a little rouge?"

"Rouge?" Clara cried, appalled. She rubbed her cheeks with her napkin showing him the results then and there. The president nodded with a weak smile and sipped the soup of his ices. Other conversations were started. Clara seemed ready to burst into tears, and blew her nose. "Come, Clara," Beril said, quickly upending his demitasse. "You're tired." They left amid a few bleak goodbyes from the dais and walked the several blocks home. Clara's feet hurt. Also, she was very hungry.

With spring of 1922 came Clara's brother and her two sisters, Sarah and Fanny, who were practically carbon copies of each other, with the same henna-red hair, flattish noses and, when they laughed, which was often, big white teeth and prominent pink gums. Of Hymie, the kid brother, it was best not to think too much. A toothpick chewer, like Alex, he was also a chain smoker, and it was all Beril could do to keep the little tin Turkish box filled. At fifteen, he was only five years older than Samuel Joseph, but Clara insisted that all the children, Samuel Joseph included, call him "Uncle." Not "Uncle Hymie," but "Uncle *Jack*," a name which had implanted itself in Hymie's mind at Ellis Island and blossomed there as the final flowering of Americanization. He too was looking for a "job," and so each morning he and Alex sauntered off to the local vegetarian cafeteria and stayed there ogling the *meydlach* until it was time to come back for lunch.

Full house? Not quite. Moses still loomed on the horizon, and Clara was pregnant. It was not a usual pregnancy in that Clara, who usually martyred herself by eating anything that was left over, suddenly began demanding strawberries, pickles, halvah, everything that her heart desired and at all hours of the day and night. Beril ran around trying to placate her, and the children thought he had gone mad. In the evening, when everything had quieted down a bit, stories of the old country were told and retold, and everyone listened like scouts around a campfire. Clara's favorite was of the death of her brother Yitzhak a few years before, and she asked for it repeatedly though each time it reduced her to a flood of tears. The usual pogrom story, it ran as follows: Sarah, Fanny, Hymie and Yitzhak and their mother were sitting in their house, chatting. Their mother smiled as she darned. It was a lovely Ukrainian springtime. They talked of America, of Clara's new husband of whom Moses had written them, of how their father would send for them soon. Their mother, who was ill, knew she would not see another spring, but did not say so. She was that kind of a mother. Suddenly, the thunderous hooves of horses were heard. They dropped what they were doing and ran into the woods to hide. Yitzhak who had gone to look for berries was left behind. Perhaps he did not hear the tumult. Sweet, blond, beloved young Yitzhak, the apple of their mother's eye. In any case, the Cossacks dismounted in the yard and demanded admittance to the house and all possible plunder. Yitzhak, unarmed and innocent, advanced toward them. Perhaps he was acting as a decoy, it was in his character. (Beril glanced at Hymie.) "What can you find here?" Yitzhak said. "We're only poor Jews." He opened his arms as if to say, see, you have nothing to gain or fear from us. Atop a horse, one of the Cossacks took aim. He was a dead shot. In the woods, the others stared through leaves and underbrush, aghast. The mother opened her mouth to cry out. Sarah clapped a hand over it. She knew she was being disrespectful, but it was the only way. The mother struggled a bit and then subsided so as not to endanger them all. They peered through the woods as the tragedy unfolded before them, steady and inexorable, like a Greek frieze. Yitzhak was still pleading, trying to distract them from what they would see over his shoulder if they only had the wits. But Cossacks had no wits, only an appetite for shooting Jews like fish in a barrel. Which was how they shot Yitzhak. The shot echoed in the countryside. Yitzhak clutched his heart and spun around, his mouth an O. "Mama!" he cried, and it was all Sarah could do to restrain her.

The Cossacks rode off in a whirl of dust, laughing and singing. The family, what was left of it, remained crouched in the woods until sunset. The mother threw herself across Yitzhak's body, and Sarah made her go to bed. "I had to put my hand over her mouth," Sarah apologized, "there was no other way." By now, the children were weeping almost as hard as Clara. She had lit two yahrzeit candles and asked Beril to say kaddish as well as Alex and Hymie, feeling it would be more effective coming from an ordained rabbi. For of course the mother had sickened and died soon after her son's murder, which made it all the worse. Sometimes Beril wondered if Clara might not have been a different person if she had stayed with her gentle mother instead of coming to America with flinty-hearted Moses. Who knew? He looked at Sarah, half-quizzical, half-amused, struck by how much this buxom red-haired sixteen-year-old girl reminded him of Clara and then again not. Where Clara wept, Sarah laughed, while Clara was still blowing her nose, Sarah was making a joke. The other, Fanny, was of somewhat coarser fiber, though also jolly. But her voice rasped and she laughed too long. Eventually rumors reached Beril via Clara's mutterings that Fanny had taken up with an Italiener. Beril pretended not to hear, even when the "Italiener" turned out to be a Greek.

It was a Chekovian summer, what with sitting around in the yard, drinking seltzer with jam in it, and telling stories. At night there were fireflies. Beril had screened in the porch, white-slatted swing and all, and Fanny and Sarah in their summer dresses rocked back and forth. Fanny, besides her Italiener, who dared not show his face, had acquired a new suitor, Harry Pollack, a cutter of men's pants, some years her senior, a wiry man with a brush mustache, as dapper as Beril but without his *yiches*.

Beril likewise. "Look at this sand!" Clara cried. "What did you expect us to bring home from the beach—latkes?" Sarah laughed. "Why didn't you come too?" "You're crazy or what?" Clara cried again. "You don't know I'm pregnant?" "Clara," Sarah said, "the whole world knows you're pregnant." There were a few more excursions to Coney Island. The aunts went on one of the rides, and Alex and Hymie strolled the boardwalk. Beril bought everyone sodas and kosher hot dogs. (That they were kosher he verified by looking up the name of the rabbi who certified them.) And once they all took a ride to Bear Mountain on the Hudson River Dayline, Clara included. Malke Leah lost her straw skimmer to the wind. "You see?" Clara said, having predicted the worst all along. "You see?"

Then a leaf fell, then another. Beril thought about fall and the High Holidays. He began to prepare for them in earnest, an undertaking that even Clara took seriously, though mostly this meant telling the children to keep quiet. Rosh Hashanah. Then Yom Kippur. Kol Nidre night they all trotted off to shul in the new finery Beril had given them money to buy, including Alex who was beginning to turn Communist. This time everybody's shoes pinched. The females deployed themselves in the balcony, the men below. Beril appeared on the bima, resplendent in his white robe, square white yarmulke, a long tallis with a brocaded silver collar. The congregation had hired a chazan, but before he commenced, Beril walked up and down the aisle with a Torah, praying, "*Or zorua latsadik*. Light is sown for the righteous," a prayer so sacred he wouldn't entrust it to anyone. When he had finished he slapped his prayer book for silence. The chazan took over. "*Kol Nidree-ay. . . .*"

Beril looked around. Everything seemed in order. The

cantor was in fine voice. The children looked awed. Clara was trying to find her place, the two aunts were flirting with a couple of young men down below, Alex and Hymie looked bored and superior. The yodelers were only a few sins ahead of the rest. *"V 'al cheyt . . .* And for the sins for which we deserve the punishment of excision, and for the sins . . ." *"S'lach lonu, m'chal lonu, kaper lonu. . . .* Forgive us, pardon us, grant us atonement." "Atonement, atonement," went the yodelers. Beril slapped the prayer book for order again, with especial attention toward the women, and began a sermon in Yiddish. At the end, the men pledged money and the women wept. The next day at each yizkor there would be three more such fund raising efforts. The new synagogue, like all synagogues, was badly in need of funds. Beril blessed them and kept them, wished them a good fast. The congregation filed out, the men first, women and children marching down from the balcony. *"Tateh,* I want to fast too," Malke Leah piped up on the way home. "You're too little." "So do I," Sarah Rachel said. "You're too young." Samuel Joseph proudly remained silent, already preoccupied with his bar mitzvah. Clara naturally had to keep up her strength because she was pregnant. They all went to bed in a dark house, their only light the yahrzeit candles flickering in the kitchen.

The next day, Yom Kippur, lasted a long time. There were endless *al cheyts*, the silent reading of the Amidah, everybody standing and swaying, rocking back and forth. At one point Beril prostrated himself at the altar. *Avinu malkeynu,* Our Father, Our King. The Cohanim, feet washed by the Levites, intoned their priestly blessing, tented by their talesim. Beril gave three sermons, each one better than the last. The pledges rolled in.

Only the yizkor itself presented a problem, and that of a domestic nature. Beril prayed for the soul of Basha, the children for the soul of their mother. Clara had not wanted them to. Why should the whole world know she was a second wife? But at this Beril had drawn the line, and even Clara had known better than to pursue it, though all during *Ne'ilah*, the last and most arduous prayer, which again Beril would not let the chazan daven but insisted on davening himself, she stood grim and tight-lipped, her prayer book closed on an index finger.

At last it was over. The cantor blew the shofar and Beril blessed them and kept them again. Clara went on ahead to bustle about the kitchen preparing the meal, taking the girls and Sarah and Fanny, who had wanted to flirt some more, along with her. Samuel Joseph remained behind, solemnly accepting the congratulations and good wishes tendered his father as if they were his own. "*Gut yom tov,* Rabbi." "*Gut yom tov.*" "*Gut yor,* Rabbi." "*Gut yor.*" Several of the balabatim assumed the honor of accompanying rabbi and son home. Rabbi and family all ate a festive meal, took short naps, then hurried back to the shul for the Yom Kippur dance. The band, a fiddle, a clarinet, and a snare drum was loud and lively. The president's wife, who had organized the event, asked Beril to dance. Clara, planted on a chair like an overstuffed pillow, looked shocked. "I haven't danced since the yeshiva," Beril said, laughing. "Very well then, but I'll ask you again." Clara, she asked nothing, having long ago stopped inviting her to join the Ladies Auxiliary, or to participate in bazaars or rummage sales, for that matter. Still, it was a pleasant evening. Fanny and Sarah had found their new swains, Alex and Hymie stalked around like two Marx Brothers, his three children slid about on the slippery resined floor, bumping into the dancers who looked down at them and laughed. It was good to see the children happy for a change. *B'rosh hashanah yikaseyvun*, Beril thought. On Rosh Hashanah it was inscribed. On Yom Kippur it was sealed. And what would his fate include for the year? Maybe a boy?

The girl, scheduled for Purim, arrived at Chanukah. Though what was her rush nobody knew. In a way, Beril held Sarah to blame except that it had all begun so innocently. They were all sitting around the dining-room table, swapping stories, eating oranges and nuts from the big bowl that was always there studded with nutcrackers. Beril had told them about parting the Red Sea kasha with chicken shmaltz, and then Sarah, urged on by Clara, who hadn't had a good cry in a long time, launched into the murder of Yitzhak. All went well until the shot rang out. Clara screamed. Even for Clara this response was somewhat exaggerated, and they all looked at her. She was now clutching her breasts, her stomach, crying, "Get the doctor!" Beril quickly called for a taxi, then looked at his watch. The *"Oy vay!"*'s were coming at ten-minute intervals. They had better hurry. Outside, it was icy and sleeting—would Clara attempt childbirth under any other conditions?—but the doctor arrived at the hospital shortly after they did. Clara was whisked away. He paced about the waiting room, sat down, stood up again. He thought of Basha and the waddling midwife. This way was better, more impersonal, more scientific, more American. But why so early? If Sarah ever told that story again, he would kill her. Finally, he saw the baby before Clara did. Two months early, weighing two and a half pounds, it was in an incubator, and looked like a poor man's chicken. Beril peered at it in its contraption through the glass. That was *his*? He hurried in to see Clara, kissed her and said, "Incubator," before she closed her eyes and drifted back to sleep, snoring lightly. "Incubator," he repeated to his family, "incubator."

After about three weeks the baby was brought home by him and Clara, wrapped and swaddled beyond recognition. Inside the wrappings it still resembled a chicken. Clara was beside herself with anxiety. "How will we manage, Beril? What will we do?" "We'll manage, we'll manage," Beril said, giving it a bottle. The first three peered into the crib. "It's a chicken," Samuel Joseph said, having been told to expect a new sister. "One more word," Beril said, "and I'll give you such a *patsh*—" "But, *tateh*, you said—" Malke Leah said, putting in her two cents' worth. "Said, said, a man says a lot in a lifetime." "Can I hold her?" Sarah Rachel asked. "Beril—!" Beril glared, held up his hand for silence, and having decided that the baby had sucked enough, proceeded to the next step, which was to wrap it in a roll of cotton wool soaked in warm olive oil. They all stared down at the tiny thing. Even the name was going to be a problem. Clara had wanted to call her Rachel after her dead mother, but there was little Sarah Rachel, still living and named after Basha's mother. "So there's more than one mother in the world," Beril said, as Clara regarded her stepdaughter bitterly. "Whose?" "*Moshe Rabeynu's*." In the Bible, the name of Moses' mother was Yocheved. Beril translated it as Julia.

In time, Julia thrived, a butterball. Clara had finally taken over her care and feeding, and Julia gained weight so steadily that if she stumbled on top of a hill, she rolled down it. When at two she got pneumonia, it was double. There was a great advent of physicians, frock coats, stethoscopes. Clara was convinced that the child would die momentarily. "Please, Clara—" "Aha!" Clara cried. "But if it was one of *your* three . . ." His three. If there had been a stepmother school, Clara would have been an A student. Ordinarily, he would have laughed the matter off with Sarah, but Sarah had recently married Harry Pollack. Beril had performed the ceremony. Out of spite, Fanny had then married the Italiener and who had performed *that* ceremony, God alone knew. To top it all off, Alex had then announced proudly that he had become a card-carrying Communist. Beril had immediately thrown him out, while Clara looked on horrified. The *meshumed* sister-in-law was bad enough, but an atheist brother-in-law he certainly didn't need around the house. Which left, as company, Hymie and also Moses, who had come up north, presented them with a large framed photograph of himself, and spent most of his time sitting under it, expecting to be waited on. The synagogue was no longer an oasis, either. In spite of the general prosperity, the money was not rolling in as expected. "They're reneging on their pledges," Beril told the president. "They promise us eighteen dollars for *chai*, and give us nine." "It's a tradition," the president said. "They always pledge more than they give. It looks better." "Tradition? Jewish tradition is that a man must honor his word. The sages tell us—"

"Rabbi," the president interrupted, sitting down in the one chair in Beril's office. "You came to us as an accomplished fund raiser."

"I'm still an accomplished fund raiser."

"No doubt. But as long as we're speaking frankly—"

The president cleared his throat, toying with a rubber band on the desk. "Well, to tell the truth, a growing community like ours needs not only an energetic rabbi, but an energetic rebbetzin as well. A modern woman, a go-getter. An *English*-speaking—" Beril did not need to hear the rest. At night, tossing and turning beside a snoring Clara, he began to have nightmares about life insurance, toilet deodorants on commission. The handwriting was on the wall. If only there were some shul where he could be independent, handle things in his own way, without the need of a helpmeet.

Still, with one hand God gave, even if with the other he took away. There was the happy occasion of Yosel's bar mitzvah, at which the boy, coached by his father, got through the whole of his Haftorah without a false note, though tone deaf, thunderingly delivered the speech Beril had written for him, and even remembered to thank everyone for their presents of fountain pens and five-dollar gold pieces. (He had also, fired by his new manhood, eaten all the jelly beans off the jelly-bean cake Clara had made for the party, and Clara had become hysterical, but that was another matter.) Best of all, Cathrael, unable to attend himself, had sent as emissary his own Samuel Joseph. There was the usual problem of names, solved by calling one son Big Joe, the other son Little Joe—just as there was a Big Sarah and a Little Sarah—but otherwise the visit was a great success. So great that Big Joe soon came back to live with them and go to NYU, and ultimately, if possible, find himself a good Jewish girl as a wife. Clara liked him, too, he called her ma'am and helped carry the coal. He also bought puzzles and games for the children, signed notes with little grinning faces that said, "Keep smiling," and played a creditable game of chess. Soon, despite the fifteen-year difference in their ages, Beril began to treat this new boarder more as a younger brother and a friend than as a nephew. He did not have Cathrael's wisdom and charm, he was sometimes silly, but a man could tell him his troubles. He was company. Together they went to the Lower East Side to buy food for the holidays, books and prizes for the Talmud Torah, saw plays on Second Avenue: Molly Picon in *Yidl Mitn Fidl*, Maurice Schwartz in *Yoshe Kalb*, Jacob Ben Ami in a Yiddish adaptation of *A Doll's House*. Not since he had been on the road, had Beril seen so many plays, and for those few exciting hours in the theater he could almost forget his worries. And once, treating the boy to tea with lemon at the Cafe Royale, he was taken by an actor to be an actor himself.

"I'm a rabbi," my father laughed.

The actor did not laugh with him.

"Orthodox Jews hate us."

"Not all, not all," my father said.

"I was even thrown out of a little shul recently when I tried to say kaddish for my father."

"The rabbi did that?"

"Not even. They don't have one. It was one of the balabatim."

"Where is this place?"

"Uptown, on Forty-seventh Street. A block or two from Broadway."

My father and Big Joe looked at each other.

The name was not promising. The West Side Hebrew Relief Association. In parenthesis (Congregation Ezrath Israel). Neither, for that matter, was the first interview, with a Mr. Alter, who pondered my father's credentials hard and long. Also, though near Broadway physically, spiritually—except for Columbia Stage Lighting and the rehearsal hall next door—the little shul was in a world of its own. A world of small home owners, butchers, grocers, dabblers in real estate. The East Side and its pushcarts was far away. Brooklyn was out of it completely. The balabatim seemed extremely conservative. They took snuff and there were spittoons in the *beth hamedresh*.

"You're right on top of Longacre Square, I see," Beril said, as Mr. Alter continued to examine his *smicha*.

"*Actyoren*," Mr. Alter said, regarding him suspiciously.

Nevertheless my father persisted. By the third or fourth interview, which took place in Mr. Alter's house, a brownstone with a ferny tree in the backyard, he had persuaded Mr. Alter and several of the other important balabatim, including an old man named Kapetsky, that not only did they need a rabbi but a Hebrew teacher in one and the same person. The salary was agreed upon, forty dollars a week in the winter, twenty dollars in the summer when the Hebrew school was out. (Mrs. Alter and her two daughters smiled at him, and he smiled back.) When he had tendered his resignation in Canarsie, with a pretense of no hard feelings on either side, he was handed a contract. It was his very first, with fine print and other impressive addenda. Next, there was the problem of housing. They took him to see an apartment on Forty-seventh Street itself, right across from the synagogue. Very convenient. That it was also six flights up and a railroad flat wasn't stressed. In his mind, Beril began to assign rooms to each member of his family as if it were Yom Kippur: who would sleep in the back bedroom, who in the front, who next to the bathroom, who in the hall, etc.

"Wouldn't the rebbetzin like to take a look before you decide?" Mrs. Alter asked. "She's not well," Beril said quickly. Not well? "I mean, she has four children." Was this a disease? Beril let the matter hang and rushed home to announce the fait accompli.

"So it's all set, Clara," he said, rubbing his hands. "We move in two weeks."

"Two weeks?" Clara said. "*Oy, vay iz mir!*"

"Clara, it's near Broadway."

The word went by her. "What about Julia?"

"We'll bundle her up."

"And Hymie?"

"He can live with Big Sarah."

"And Big Joe?"

"He'll stay in a dormitory and come to visit."

"And Zayde?"

He had forgotten about his father-in-law. He looked into the living room where Moses sat under his photograph, waiting to play casino.

"That's the best part," Beril said. "We'll partition him among his children. A month here, a month there. That way he gets to see everybody."

For a moment, Clara seemed mollified.

"You see? I told you not to worry."

"Don't *worry*?" Clara cried to empty air, for he had gone off to tell the children.

Moving day came and went. Clara fell to pieces with her first sight of the new apartment, and viewing it from her eyes, he could hardly blame her. It was dark, long and narrow, and smelled of gas. Downstairs, men loitered in the hallway, a potential menace to Sarah Rachel and

Malke Leah, and also Julia, if she should ever lose weight. Across the street was P.S. 17 where he would enroll them, and in its Gothic shadow, the little shul. Beril assumed his new duties. The spittoons in the *beth hamedresh* still bothered him. The little office upstairs was a two-by-four, with hardly enough room for his robes and talesim, much less his newly acquired Hebrew typewriter, which he decided to leave at home. The stationery was so crowded with the names of balabatim, it was hard to imagine getting a word in edgewise, anyway. There were definitely changes to be made. Shaking his head, he started toward the stairs to conduct services, and as he descended met a young man in greasepaint leaving. He remembered that it was Wednesday.

"Where are you going?" Beril said. "You have time before the evening performance."

"The rabbi said I couldn't say kaddish for my father here."

"Who said that?"

The actor pointed to old man Kapetsky, praying violently among the other congregants.

"*I'm* the rabbi here," Beril said, taking him back in and giving him a prayer book. He turned to the page with the kaddish, and when the time came to say it, enunciated the words so loudly and distinctly even the proprietor of the spaghetti parlor down the street could have followed him. Mr. Kapetsky was glaring daggers.

"*Yisgadal v'yiskadash sh'mey rabo. . . .*" The actor had said he was in Florenz Ziegfeld's new musical with Eddie Cantor. Ziegfeld, my father repeated to himself, Cantor. "*B'ol mo divro chirusey. . . .*"

II
FORTY~
SEVENTH
STREET

"*V'yamlich malchusey* . . ."

On a Friday morning in October, two years later, my father sat in his tiny office right after services, glumly pondering the contents of his collection box. The High Holidays had come and gone, but his mind was still concerned with credits and debits. Inside the *pushke*, which the shammos had just passed around, nickels and dimes, as usual it came to nothing. Neither did the eleven dollars a year membership fee. On a higher plane, he thought, rolling the coins in papers for the bank, there was not much to boast about either. His contract was soon to expire, and with it most of his dreams of making a hit in this place. Red, the young man he had saved from Mr. Kapetsky, was still the only actor who came to shul regularly, though sometimes accompanied by a friend with a dog act, or a songwriter from Tin Pan Alley. For the rest of it, all he had managed to do was squeeze his name onto the stationery, get rid of the spittoons in the *beth hamedresh*, stop the sale of *aliyahs* to the Torah—"Mr. Kapetsky, being called to the Torah is an honor, not a bargain." And, if one wanted to consider it an accomplishment, sire a fourth daughter, Channele—me.

Of course, he consoled himself, Eddie Cantor had five and even made jokes on the subject. But to Clara, who had not wanted another baby in the first place, it was no laughing matter. A breech birth, she often cried, the sure sign of a troublemaker. Not to mention the fact of still another girl in a neighborhood where even the greatest beauty would have trouble finding a good Jewish husband. Still, to his surprise, he had taken to his new baby at once. Blond, green-eyed, I might have been a gift from the *goldene medina*, and if in addition to my mother's looks I should also have my father's brains, who knew what might happen? And hadn't 1927 so far been a year of notable events in general? A year in which Lindbergh had flown the Atlantic, Sacco and Vanzetti been executed, and Al Jolson, a Jew, appeared in the first talking picture?

Sighing, my father stuck the rolls of coins into the top drawer of his desk. Unfortunately, to his balabatim as well as to Clara, 1927 was also not a year to shout about. Going their way just as if he weren't there, they still pledged at yizkors not twice but three times what they meant to deliver, sent their children to the Talmud Torah but ignored the bills for tuition, prayed loud and long at evening services but in the mornings went straight to their businesses. The morning minyans at the West Side Hebrew Relief Association, to tell the truth, had become my father's chief torment. Each day he entered the *beth hamedresh* praying in advance that he would find ten men. When he didn't, he was forced to send the shammos, a dolt from the old country whom he had inherited along with the spittoons, out on Forty-seventh Street to scout around. One day this genius had come in dragging a gray-bearded gentleman who had protested all the way to the ark. "*Shah!* What kind of a Jew makes such a noise?" the shammos had demanded. In answer the old man had hysterically lifted his beard to reveal an enormous silver crucifix. "*Oy, gevald!*" the shammos had cried, retreating in terror. My father wearily sent the Greek Orthodox priest on his way. Another morning, counting to eight, he had sent the shammos over to the police station to get a couple of Jewish detectives. The shammos had returned with two prisoners. *Dayenu.* But in handcuffs?

No, there was not much to boast about, and soon Clara would come to leave the baby while she did her shabbos marketing and tell him of some fresh catastrophe. Julia had tried to send little Channele down in the dumbwaiter. Julia had left the baby on a window ledge and opened the window. Each time, luckily, Sarah Rachel, a sweet-natured child, had come to the rescue, but who knew how long this luck would last? Then, after Clara, there would be an appointment on a very delicate matter with Miss Bohan, the principal of P.S. 17 next door, a Tammany appointee who had barely finished normal school, and who could not seem to appreciate the special needs and feelings of her few Jewish students, including Sarah

Rachel and Mildred (née Malke Leah), who were both enrolled there. Yosel was in De Witt Clinton High School, already planning to major in journalism at NYU like his cousin and namesake, Big Joe. Not such a bad idea, since the boy's froglike singing voice that had barely made it through his bar mitzvah would alone preclude his being a rabbi. Except that NYU cost money, and my father had no idea where he would find it. Sighing again, he put the problem aside and decided to use these few moments of peace to make some notes on his sermon for tomorrow, transcribing them at home later on his Hebrew typewriter. Holidays notwithstanding, each Saturday morning he was expected to deliver an inspirational sermon, a *drosha* of the highest order, even if they all dozed through it.

"The Jews," he jotted down, thinking a moment, "are a nation of dreamers. . . ." There was a familiar disruption from downstairs, which he chose to ignore. "Our dreams are not only our personal history, but enable us to create a life for ourselves in exile. . . ." The downstairs door opened again, and some local children playing hooky ran in screaming "Kike!" and "Sheeny!" He chased them away with a broomstick he kept handy for the purpose, returned to his tiny office, and thought some more. "Individual Jews get respect, but for the Jewish masses, the doors are locked. As it was in Egypt, so it is in America. . . ."

A determined clomping up the stairs interrupted this latest installment. He pushed away his notes.

"Beril!"

"Good morning, Clara."

She dumped me on his desk and he put his arm around

my waist and handed me a paper flag left over from Simchas Torah to play with.

"Tonight is shabbos."

"I know that."

"Zayde's coming for a month."

"I know that too."

She looked at him with the intense concentration of a
cardplayer trying to decide whether to play a trump.
The years had not been kind to Clara, nor she to them.
From plump, she had become stout. Gone was the honey
plait and in its stead she wore a boyish "personality" bob
with a spitcurl on each cheek fashioned by a barber on
Ninth Avenue under the El. Only the housedresses had
remained the same day in and day out, flowered wrap-
arounds that expanded with her increasing girth and over
which, if it was cold like today, she threw an old black
coat. Holding her black pocketbook and empty shopping
bag against her stomach, she watched him helping me
wave my flag. "Careful, darling, don't poke my eyes out."

"Julia's nose is running," she said finally, putting a foot
into troubled waters.

"So keep her home from kindergarten."

"I can't. Sarah already took her."

"Okay, I'll bring her back. Anything else?"

"Sarah needs an eye operation."

"Clara, again with the eye operation?"

"I'm telling you no boy will look at her unless she gets
it fixed."

"Have a heart, Clara. Have a little *rachmones*. The kid's
only in the eighth grade."

"And Mildred is in the sixth grade."

"So?"

"So she talks a mile a minute. It's not natural."

"Believe me, she won't be the first Jewish wife with that affliction," my father said, digging into his pocket for a few dollars, enough he hoped, for Clara to stuff her shopping bag with soup greens, carp, whitefish, pickles, chicken and whatever else she wanted to get for Friday night. Otherwise, there would be still more items on the long penciled chit held by Mr. Harkevy, the grocer.

When she had gone off, having first opened and closed her mouth futilely several times, like a carp, he carefully undid the paper flag from my fist and took me on his lap, smoothing out my pink baby coat and bonnet. Julia, she stuffed like a goose. Me, she dressed like a doll, furious if anyone got me *shmutzik*, still her favorite word. He looked around for something clean to play with and picked up the *Jewish Daily Forward*, resting his chin on my head as he pointed to the pictures in the sepia section. "You see, Channele, this is our mute President, the *shtimeh* Calvin Coolidge. . . . And here is our playboy mayor, James J. Walker. . . . And this is Lucky Lindy. . . . And this," moistening a finger and turning a few pages, "is the noted actress, Bessie Thomashevsky." The finger arrested itself. There was to be a benefit for her the following week, with many stars of the Jewish stage participating, including Celia Adler and Muni Weisenfreund (now Paul Muni), all performing scenes from their greatest triumphs. It would be a gala evening. He decided to take Big Joe, since they had so much enjoyed themselves at *The Jazz Singer*, and Clara never cared for a good time anyway, and folded up the paper. But something about that notice was nagging at him, something was making him respond like a firehorse to a bell, and he didn't know what. Maybe that attractive word, *benefit*? Benefits were certainly a traditional way of raising money for Jewish causes. Though it was out of the question that the stars of Second Avenue would come trooping all the way uptown to help balance the budget of this little shul. And not that with his balabatim Broadway seemed any nearer than Second Avenue at the moment. . . . Still. . . . Burrowing his chin deeper into the top of my head, he picked up and reread the notes of his sermon. "The Jews are a nation of dreamers, Channele," he said. "Did you know that?"

But first things first. After Clara had returned to claim me, reminding him once more about Julia's runny nose, he put on his hat and coat, slipped his yarmulke into his side pocket and went next door. The outer courtyard of P.S. 17 was cold and windy, the inner one smelled of sour milk. Long lines of silent children shuffled their feet like prisoners, moving slowly forward at the clang of a bell. He sat down in the anteroom of the principal's office, with one deft motion removed his hat and slipped on his yarmulke, then waited. The door finally opened, and Miss Bohan appeared, a thin woman with reddish gray hair and a face like a pale wrinkled prune.

"Good morning, Rabbi," she said, without inviting him in.

"Good morning," he answered, rising.

"And what can I do for you today?"

"Well," my father began with a little smile, "a small problem has come up."

"Again?"

"There haven't been so many."

"You know, Rabbi," Miss Bohan said, "until you appeared, we hadn't realized that the needs of our Jewish pupils were so special. But now it appears to be one thing after another."

"It just seems like that," my father said.

"We now allow the Jewish children not to bow their heads during the blessing at assemblies."

"Jews don't bow their heads except in the synagogue. It's part of our heritage."

"We acceded to your request that the Bible reading each morning be restricted to the Old Testament."

"It's your Testament too."

"We have permitted the Jewish children to remain silent when Christmas carols are sung, even though some of them stick out their tongues and make faces in the process."

Seymour Katz. "Give me the names of the offenders and I'll take care of them," my father said.

"The Jewish children no longer collect for the Red Cross because—as you pointed out—there is a cross in Red Cross. They also do not eat what they make in cooking class, though the other children are stuck with it and even Mrs. Sinsheimer who is a Jew herself doesn't understand."

Mrs. Sinsheimer was a *German* Jew, a horse of another color, my father thought but didn't say. "It's very simple," he remarked, smiling again. "The children are allowed to cook unkosher food, they just can't eat it."

"And now what?"

My father paused. The mission was indeed delicate and he wanted to be careful how he went about it. "It's Mrs. Sinsheimer again."

"Again?"

"My daughters tell me she's introduced some personal

articles of her own into the laundry class for demonstration purposes."

"I beg your pardon?"

Another pause. "I love this country," my father said. "I'm not only a citizen, I'm a registered Democrat. So are most of my constituents—I mean, congregation."

Miss Bohan's mean little Irish eyes got meaner.

"And so I ask you, in a democracy is it fair that some people should wash other people's bloomers?"

"I'll take care of it," Miss Bohan said.

"Thank you," my father said, replacing his yarmulke with his hat. "And give my regards to your brother, the Judge."

Mission accomplished, he hauled a protesting Julia from kindergarten and pushed her up six evil-smelling flights to deposit her in the railroad flat with Clara, who immediately stopped braiding a challah to blow Julia's nose with one of his handkerchiefs. At Clara's urging, he took Julia's temperature (normal), ate some pot cheese and sour cream standing up, chucked me under the chin as I lay in my crib in the kitchen, and returned to the synagogue, where he opened the mail and toted up all the week's receipts on an abacus. Since there was no Hebrew school on Friday afternoons (he would give Seymour Katz a piece of his mind on Monday), he had time to make a careful accounting before he made a dash for the bank, leaving the shammos in charge with the broomstick. As he stood on line between Mr. Plotkin, of dry goods and kiddie togs, and Mr. Klein, the local kosher butcher, whose thumb frequently weighted down the scales along with his brisket, an immediate application of Saturday's sermon occurred to him. Back in shul, he reread the notice about Bessie Thomashevsky several times, and between afternoon and evening services, *mincha* and *maariv*, had made up his mind what he wanted to do.

"*Gut shabbos*, Rabbi."

"*Gut shabbos*, Mr. Alter. And how are your wife and daughters?"

"Fine, thank God. Mrs. Alter would like to know when you and Mrs. Birstein are coming over."

"Soon," my father said. "Very soon. As soon as my wife feels better."

"*Gut shabbos*, Rabbi."

"*Gut shabbos*, Mr. Goldman. And how is Mendel's head feeling since his operation?"

"He has a big scar."

"Better a scar than a *veytig*," my father said.

"*Gut shabbos—Rabbi*."

"*Gut shabbos—Mister* Kapetsky. . . . *Gut shabbos—* oh, Red! It's good to see you back in town. How was the road?"

"You know how it is," Red said. "Drafty trains and awful boarding houses." Red did look tired. His redhead's skin, milky white to begin with, now looked as if the boyish freckles had been painted on it.

"Sometimes I think actors are the real wandering Jews," my father said, shaking his head. He drew the young man aside as the rest of the congregation filed out.

"Let me ask you an important question. Who, in your opinion, is the greatest Jewish star on Broadway today?"

"I don't know. Jolson's out on the coast. Eddie Cantor? Sophie Tucker?"

"All right," my father said. "We'll start with her."

"Start what with her?" Red asked.

"Our benefit. I've decided to have a benefit in December, right after Chanukah."

"A benefit right after Chanukah?"

"We'll ask the greatest stars in show business to donate their talents," my father said, with a sweep of his arm. "With Sophie, it will be a smash."

"Rabbi, she's a nice lady, but she doesn't play benefits."

"Did you ever ask her?"

"Of course not, but—"

"Where's she playing?"

"At the Music Box. But listen, Rabbi, it won't do you any good."

"Red, Red," my father said. "You're forgetting your Jewish history. Do you think among the Maccabees there was such a word as *defeat*? Of course, I'm going to need your help."

It would perhaps have been easier if Clara were not acting as if he were going to Siberia instead of just down a few streets. "*Shabbos bay nacht?*" she cried. "*Du bist meshuga?* It's late. It's cold. Zayde wants to play dominoes."

He carefully put aside the braided *havdalah* candle and the spice shaker with which he had just finished saying good-bye to the sabbath bride. At the chipped enamel table, Mildred sat with her mouth open, silent for once, Yosel put down his book, Zayde looked up from trying to find a dotted double six, Sarah Rachel let me slip back into my high chair, and Julia in her corkscrew curls and smocked blue dress stopped putting shmaltz on another piece of pumpernickel.

"Calm yourself," my father said. "I'll be back in half an

dazzled him. There were bright lights everywhere. No wonder they called it the Great White Way. News bulletins flashed in the Times Tower. The great striped fish in the Wrigley sign swam in a squiggly sea. Light bulbs rimmed the square theater marquees, illuminating the Palace, the Loew's State, the Strand, the Ziegfeld Follies, Helen Hayes in *Coquette*, George White's *Scandals*, *Abie's Irish Rose*, *Funny Face* with Adele and Fred Astaire. For a moment he forgot everything, taxis, playgoers, news vendors, Clara, *tsuris*, balabatim, everything, except that once he had wanted to run away and be an actor himself.

He had never been inside a legitimate Broadway theater before, much less backstage. Sophie Tucker refused to see him. The man he had sent with the first message, came back with another. "She said to tell you to go away. She said she's going on in a few minutes and not to be here when she gets off." "Tell her I'll enjoy the show from here," my father said, looking around vainly for a place to sit down and finally backing up against a wall. There was a great deal of hurry and movement, people shifting scenery, calling time. For all the attention he attracted he might have been a piece of scenery himself. From the dark distant recesses of the theater, the orchestra music resounded and came to a crashing climax. There was a burst of applause. A long line of skinny chorus girls came prancing by, all half-naked, the taller ones with plumes in their hair to make them look still taller. A far cry from the *zaftik*, gold-toothed grandmothers clomping away in Yiddish musicals. It was a good thing Clara wasn't around to urge them to bundle up. Then the great star, Sophie

Tucker herself, emerged from a dressing room and rushed past him. The Last of the Red Hot Mamas, as she billed herself, dressed in a gleaming satin gown that, even color-blind, he knew was bright red. She was enormously fat, but like the chorus girls also wore a giant plume in her blond pompadour. He edged nearer the wings, now able to see her onstage in profile. "Some of these days," she sang in a low growling voice, caught by a single spotlight, "you're gonna miss me, honey. Some of these days, you're gonna feel so blue. You'll miss my lovin', you'll miss my kissin', you'll miss my . . ." From this, bowing deeply, ample bosom and all, she went on to, "Shine on, shine on, harvest moon, up in the sky"—she looked up at the balcony—"I ain't had no lovin' since January, February, June and July. . . ." And from there, eventually, thank God, to "*Mein Yiddishe Mameh.*" As the last notes sank deep into her throat, there was a momentary hush, then a burst of applause. The stage went black. He stationed himself near the door of her starred dressing room.

"Miss Tucker—" he said, doffing hat and donning yarmulke. "I'm Rabbi Birstein."

"Rabbi?" she said, giving him a quick backward glance. "You look like an unemployed juvenile."

"Why unemployed?" my father asked, following her inside.

"Because with that scarf hanging out of your pocket— no, forget it," she sighed, powdering her sweaty face and glistening exposed bosom with a huge pink puff. She leaned over the cluttered dressing table and peered at herself in a mirror surrounded by light bulbs, then beckoned to her Negro dresser. "Look, whoever you are, I'm going on in a few minutes. If it's a contribution you want, see my manager."

"The contribution I want isn't money."

"No?" she said, retiring behind a screen. "What is it then?"

"You," my father said, drawing up a chair uninvited. "Let me level with you, Miss Tucker. My shul is at present mortgaged to the ears."

"Which shul—?"

"The West Side Hebrew Relief Association, also known as Congregation Ezrath Israel."

"That's some name—Josephine, hand me that drink, please."

"You're a clever woman, Sophie, which is why I felt I could appeal to you in the first place." "Hey, watch out for my hair!" "Because the way I see the situation is this. We're on Forty-seventh and Eighth, a block from Broadway. I want actors to come to us, to feel welcome for a change. I want it to be *their* shul."

"An actors synagogue?"

"A haven," my father said. "A temple."

"So what do you want from me?"

He told her.

"No, I'm sorry," she said, emerging from behind the screen, "I don't play benefits." He rose and looked up at her. She was wearing a different red gown, even more elaborate and exposing more of her bosom than the first. Her large body shimmered with bugle beads. Her eyelids were bright blue, her cheeks heavily rouged. *Two* giant red plumes swayed atop her shiny blond hair. "What's the matter?" she said.

"Nothing."

"Why are you looking at me like that?"

"Sophie," he said, allowing a sigh to escape him, "*du bist eppes* a star, no?"

"So?"

"So tell me, who says kaddish for this 'yiddishe mameh' you're crying about? This mother of a star?"

"I suppose my brother."

"And for you, if God forbid, something should happen—you should live to be a hundred and twenty?"

"I guess my son, Bert."

"You guess?"

She looked down at him waveringly.

"Sophele," he said, pointing an index finger at her shimmering middle. "Stars don't guess. They don't suppose. They know. That's what makes them stars. The sages tell us . . ."

He paused for a moment, then shook his head, and replaced his yarmulke with his hat.

"No," he said. "You also sing about being a woman alone. I don't want to add to your burdens. Your mother will understand. I'm sure she does already."

"Hey, wait a minute," she began. "My mother will what—?" and took a quick swig of her drink. As she looked down at him again, tears suddenly sprang into her mascaraed blue eyes, and she put her drink aside. "Oy, rebele," she said in that deep throaty voice, "God damn it, I am a woman alone."

From Sophie came a promise to appear if he ever got his show together, which speaking frankly and dabbing at her eyes, she doubted would ever happen, plus a note of introduction in a florid hand to Eddie Cantor. From Eddie Cantor, popeyed and sweet-spoken, commiserations about all the daughters, regrets that Chanukah would find him in Hollywood, and a call to Smith and Dale, who said sure, they'd do one of their routines. From Red, the dog act, a pair of ballroom dancers, a family of Turkish acrobats, and an inquiry about where my father meant to put them all. "You don't want a dark house, Rabbi." "God forbid." "No, you want a big musical comedy theater that they'll let you use free on a Sunday night." "So who owns the most musical comedy theaters?" "The Shuberts, but they'll never—" From Lee Shubert, who was having terrible aggravation from his brother, came the Majestic, and with the Majestic an empty orchestra pit, a strong stagehands union, and blocks of varicolored tickets to riffle through and try to sell.

Some of the balabatim were furious, not least old man Kapetsky, who came storming into the tiny office one afternoon with an order blank in his hand.

"What is this? Suddenly this shul is called 'The Actors Temple'?"

"I put it in quotation marks."

"It's a *shandeh*!" the old man cried, slamming the desk with his fist. "A shame and a disgrace. And on top of everything else we should pay money to see some *nafkes* prancing around naked and barefoot?"

"They're not barefoot," my father said.

Mr. Kapetsky spat to one side.

"Please, Mr. Kapetsky. What do you want from actors? They're people. They need our help, and we need theirs."

. . . "Like a *loch in kop*." . . . "If you could only look on this as a cooperative venture. May I point out that our president, Mr. Alter, bought a whole block of seats?"

"Mr. Alter?" Kapetsky laughed. "Mr. Alter's wife tells him what to do."

" 'If your wife is short, bend down and listen to her,' the sages tell us," my father said, realizing too late that while he had just paid Clara an inadvertent compliment, he had forgotten that the stentorian-voiced Mrs. Kapetsky towered above her little *"tatele,"* as she called him.

"A rabbi should concern himself with Purim plays, not show business," *tatele* said.

"On Forty-seventh Street, both. Both. That's the beautiful part of it. Didn't you think Gussie Goldman made a wonderful Vashti in the play I wrote last year?"

"Because you encouraged her. Because you're letting girls into the Talmud Torah to fill up the enrollment."

"So what's the harm if they learn a little Hebrew?"

"The harm is that they only need to know how to be good Jewish wives and mothers, that's all. You're giving them ideas. You've already given everybody too many ideas. Where is God in all this, I want to know? Where is God?"

"I'll tell you a story," my father said. "Once in Kovno, there was a poor ordinary carpenter who wore his *tfiln* constantly and davened around the clock. Such a *tsadik*, everybody said. But Rabbi Israel disagreed. If that man really believed in God, he said, he would daven a little less and help other Jews a little more."

"Which means?" Mr. Kapetsky said.

"I don't believe in your kind of piety."

"And I don't believe you're a rabbi," Mr. Kapetsky said. "One of these days we'll see who's right."

Mr. Kapetsky was not the only one with grave misgivings. There was Rosen, the rug and linoleum dealer, Plotkin of dry goods and kiddie togs, Meltzer with his hops and brews, Hirscheim the glazier. A worrisome development, especially since the contract was soon to expire. Also, the more pious they were, the more sacramental wine they seemed to imbibe, and an embarrassing correspondence with Mayor Walker on the subject of Prohibition ensued. "Cheer up," Red said. "You're doing fine. You picked up three acts at the Palace last week." But that was only the half of it, and when Kapetsky's son Ely got married, the old man watched my father like a hawk as he performed the ceremony. He continued with his weddings and bar mitzvahs and funerals, taught Hebrew school, conducted services, ruled on diseased chickens, and in between peddled his theater tickets with a heavy heart, canvassing the block and beyond, selling them to Professor Mazocchi, to Columbia Stage Lighting, to Kelly in his candy store, to the poker-playing detectives at the Sixteenth Precinct, to some firemen, to Miss Bohan's brother, the Judge, to Congressman Michael J. Kennedy, to Dominick in Clara's fish store, to the pastor of the Lutheran church, whose verdigrised spire jutted into the sky above a long row of speakeasies on Forty-sixth Street. Red unloaded some more at the Friars Club, assuring the members that they would always be welcomed by the little rabbi on Forty-seventh Street.

As the eight days of Chanukah came, then went, my father's throat grew dry and his hands trembled—could this be stage fright?—and on the Sunday night of the benefit his wing collar kept flying open. Clara of course was no help. She was too busy pulling on her famous royal blue evening dress, and whipping Yosel and the two older girls into shape. Julia, who had diarrhea, and I, the baby, were being left behind in the care of Mrs. Mazocchi. He took a taxi to the theater, unloaded his brood into a box, and went backstage, having been to enough backstages by now to know the right door. The audience was beginning to fill the theater, the orchestra was tuning up in the pit. He stationed himself in the wings to watch the show. Red, acting as emcee, told a few bad jokes, and introduced his friend's dog act, which was terrible. There was nothing Jewish about a dog to begin with, including the world-renowned Rin Tin Tin, and even these foolish ones dressed in tutus and walking around on their hind legs smacked of repression and the czar. The dance team were no Castles. The Turkish acrobats, dressed in pink tights and spangles, performing each somersault and shoulder leap to a terrifying roll of drums, were even worse. He was glad none of the old-timers had come to see this fiasco. What had he done? He felt sick in the pit of his stomach.

More people in heavy stage makeup and costumes passed by him. He was aware of laughter, applause. Then Smith and Dale went onstage dressed as doctor and patient. "Dr. Kronkhite, what's the best place for rheumatism?" "Switzerland, that's where I got mine." Then Buck and Bubbles. And the Old Maestro, Ben Bernie, bringing his whole band onstage. And Pat Rooney, doing a soft shoe to "The Daughter of Rosie O'Grady." And Clayton, Jackson and Durante, fresh from the Parody Club. "Ink a dink a doo." Was it possible the show was a hit? That he was standing in his own backstage? The rest of it passed in a dream. Actors said hello to him as they came off, as if they knew him. And Sophie Tucker gave him a big hug and a kiss before she went onstage to close the show, the smash finish he had dreamed about, after several encores singing, *"Mein Yiddishe Mameh"*—"as our little rabbi has requested." Vast applause. His family was beaming in the box. It was over. What? Red gave him a little push. "You're *on*, you're *on*." He tripped out of the wings, collected himself, adjusted his wing collar and black bow tie, and walked to center stage. The orchestra music surged up. "A pretty girl is like a melodee...." The footlights dazzled him. The pale faces of the audience swam before him in the darkness. My father took a bow.

His contract was renewed, and two rocky years later renewed again. But each time after such an acrimonious meeting of the Board of Officers, to which my father listened outside with his good ear, that the memory of the invective made him wince. It did not seem to matter how often he tried to point out to Kapetsky and his crew that the benefits and their souvenir journals doubled the shul's annual income, or that, hearing of the synagogue, more and more people were coming to services and enrolling their children in the Talmud Torah. All they ever said was, "actyoren." And of course, the Crash (another lovely English word) had not made matters easier.

Still, as we sat in Big Sarah's house one Sunday afternoon in 1930, and my father read me the ads from the latest journal, there was an undeniable pride in his voice as he named the famous stars, the new lights of his life if also the bane of his existence.

"You see, Channele? 'Best wishes, Al Jolson.' 'Kind regards, Ted and Adah Lewis.' 'From Dr. Kronkhite and his only living patient.' 'To my favorite rabbi, Bill Robinson.' Next year, I'll take you backstage."

"They all come to shul?" Big Sarah asked.

"Not *Bill* Robinson, Edward G."

"Little Caesar comes to shul?"

"Definitely. I let him conduct services one morning. He was wearing his father's wool tallis."

"Imagine."

"So if you know so many famous celebrities," Hymie said in a wheedling voice, shifting his toothpick from one side of his mouth to the other, and gazing fondly at his bleached-blond wife of a few months, Goldie, an "exotic" dancer, "why can't you get her a job?"

"Because there aren't any jobs these days," my father said, though in fact Hymie had found himself one, playing the horses.

"But she's a regular Jean Harlow."

"I'll bear that in mind."

"No, Jack, he's right," Goldie said, smiling at my father with her long teeth, devoted to him ever since he had performed her wedding, and herself so horse-faced it was easy to see why Hymie had fallen in love with her. "Nobody can make a living at anything anymore."

"There is no living, there is no *parnoseh*," Harry Pollack said, looking up from the card table, long laid-off and, despite the brush mustache, no longer dapper. He had also, like the sport he once was, invested his life savings in the stock market—something my father had secretly longed to do, except that with his family and assorted hangers-on there were no life savings—and lost every penny.

"*Oy, parnoseh*," my mother echoed him, sighing so deeply I slid off her lap and went to climb up on Big Sarah's.

"So was it better in Russia?" Big Sarah laughed, revealing her lovely pink gums. "We were all dying of malnutrition. We didn't have what to eat. By the way, why is Channele so skinny?"

"Because she's skinny," my mother said. "You're still going every day to that cafeteria?"

"Dubrow's? Sure. Why not?"

"I thought maybe it cost too much money."

"For a cup of coffee and a roll? Don't be foolish, Clara. It's a nice place. I meet all my friends."

"Friends," Harry Pollack said.

"Sarah," my father sighed, "can you maybe give me another glass of tea? Then, Clara, we have to go."

"Where are you running?" Sarah said, removing me from her lap and going off to the kitchen. "You just got here."

"I have to be back for services."

"How about another hand of pinochle?" Harry Pollack suggested.

"No, really, Harry, I must run. With my shammos—"

"Beril is a nervouser," my mother said proudly, crossing her legs at the ankles an inch or two from the floor, while my father drummed his fingers on the arm of his chair. All of Big Sarah's furniture matched, a wine satin suite with dark embossed flowers. In her bedroom, an old-fashioned doll in a green satin bonnet and hoopskirt sat on the bed under a light with a rosy glow. Nevertheless, my mother was forced to admit that in spite of her romantic nature, Sarah was a *berye* too, and referred approvingly to the time we had come a half hour early and found her on her hands and knees scrubbing the bathroom floor.

"Here, Beril," Big Sarah said, returning with a glass of tea with lemon and suggesting also a piece of fruit or sponge cake, which were refused. She sat down on her sofa and smiled at him. I climbed back up on her lap and buried my nose in her soft, pink, perfumed neck.

"You smell nice," I said.

"Stop bothering her."

"She's not bothering me, Clara. What's to bother? She's light as a feather. She doesn't weigh anything."

"So if she doesn't eat," my mother said, "what should I do? Kill myself?"

"She ate here."

"Kosher frankfurters. That's not a life."

"You can only get them in a Jewish neighborhood. That's why it's such a big treat for her."

"New York has different treats," my mother said.

At the other end of the sofa, Julia put down a copy of one of Big Sarah's movie magazines, and sniffed haughtily. Sarah's little boy, Morty, was playing at her feet in his rompers, trying to tie the red satin ribbon which had come on our gift box of candy around his neck. He was exactly nine months younger than I. "I looked at Channele and got the bright idea," Big Sarah always said, winking at my father, adding proudly that Morty had eyelashes like a girl.

"Beril gives her cognac with a raw egg in it every day," my mother said defensively.

"Cognac for such a little thing?"

"Beril knows."

"Oh, Clara," Big Sarah said, shaking her head cheerfully. "It could be black as night but if Beril said it was day, it would be day."

"Days can be black, too," my father said, laughing. "Think of the plagues."

"A plague on Hoover," Harry Pollack said. "A *makeh af* Hoover."

"Amen," my father said. "Come, Clara, come Channele, come Julia."

"And the girls?" Big Sarah said, standing up.

"She likes that her aunt's hair gets redder every time we come over? She likes that her aunt sits in cafeterias looking for men?"

"She's your sister, not mine," my father said, and escaped across the street to the shul where, in spite of his increasing miseries with old man Kapetsky, now joined by his son, Ely, an even more vicious and vociferous antagonist, it was still better than at home. The truth was that he did not know how long he would be able to keep Yosel at NYU, or if the girls would be able to attend college at all. It broke his heart that Sarah, at sixteen, would have to go to work as soon as she finished high school, that Mildred would also wind up being a secretary or a file clerk, that Clara, for whom he had meant to buy furs and finery, had sent an envelope via Julia with her wedding ring inside for him to pawn. He had sent it back and stalked out of the house.

Nevertheless, with all of it, he remembered his promise to me, and at the next benefit led me backstage, all dressed up in the pink taffeta kiddie evening dress my mother had got on credit at Plotkin's, and introduced me to Belle Baker, Borah Minevitch and his Harmonica Rascals, with special attention to the dwarf, who was about my size, and George Givot, the Greek, who had just finished doing a routine based on "Yes, We Have No Bananas." My father let me watch a piece of the show from the wings, keeping his hands on my shoulders, and then returned me back down the dark carpeted aisle to the rest of the family. "This isn't your first time in a box, you know," he whispered, parting the red velvet curtains. "It isn't, Daddy?" "No, no. At *Fine and Dandy*, Joe Cook himself stopped the show and waved to you." "Really, Daddy?" "Shsh." Onstage, Georgie Jessel was singing,

{110}

"One bright and guiding light/That taught me wrong from right/I found in my mother's eyes." My mother turned around with tears streaming down her face. In the gilt chair beside her, Julia in her corkscrew curls and pink angora sweater was squirming with jealousy. But my mother had heard that the backstage was drafty.

The next spring I outpointed Julia completely by having an emergency appendectomy on my fourth birthday, which counted a lot more, in terms of aggravation, than even Julia's double pneumonia. To make matters still more impressive, the surgeon was a Gentile, and my father, not wanting to see his child in a ward, borrowed heavily against his salary to get me a private room at Roosevelt Hospital, where he brought me an endless series of toys and dolls, and my mother blew her nose tragically into his large white handkerchief.

"Clara, the operation is over. It was a success."

"Who knows what still could happen? She didn't even want to get born."

"She did, she did. She only wanted to put a toe in first. When you consider the state of the world, that's reasonable."

"It's reasonable my hair is white from aggravation?"

"Your hair turned white gradually from natural causes. You just happened to notice it."

"Naturally causes," my mother said bitterly.

Red sent me a dozen American Beauty roses in a long box. I no longer wanted any flowers except in a long box. "She's acting like a star," my father mused, and cast me in his next Purim play where my line was, "Hang Haman, hang Haman from a tree."

*   *   *

At shul my name was Channele, "the Rabbi's Channele." At home, Chanie. On the street, by extension and because the Gentile neighbors hadn't heard right, Honey. At P.S. 17, where my father ultimately enrolled me in the first grade—"Miss Bohan, what could I do? She was too smart for kindergarten"—it was Anna all the way. "She'll never go, I'm telling you," my mother said. "This one likes to sleep late." Which was true. "So Sarah will take her," my father said. And she did, buttoning me into my little coat each morning after my breakfast of coffee and a bagel, handing me my schoolbag, and walking me the four long blocks to P.S. 17. (We had moved to an elevator apartment on Fifty-first Street, near Madison Square Garden, a step up in the world, though still no palace. Pimps and whores ambled down the street, drunks lounged in the doorways, but it was still better than the railroad flat.) At the foot of the grim stone school steps, Sarah left me to continue on to her new job at the Film Center, her boss a recent addition to the congregation. The small warm shul was right next door to P.S. 17, but school was always wintery. A place of clanging bells, lines in size places, the smell of sour free lunches, daily inspections at the classroom window for nits and eczema, lessons in arithmetic, report cards. Eventually, Miss Riordan made me crayon monitor. "She knows whose daughter you are," my father said.

Sarah Rachel's name had also undergone a sea change. Reasoning that having been born in Atlanta she must be southern, she had decided to call herself Dixie and answered all questions requiring an affirmative with the word *yuh-ass*. ("Beril, what kind of a language is this?" Clara cried.) Days she worked for Republic Pictures, distributing reissues of *Hell's Angels*, *Scarface*, old Westerns, B movies, C movies, and (it was better not to dwell on this) blue movies, though like a good girl she came home each noon for Clara's blintzes or cabbage borscht. Nights, she went to Hunter College, and on weekends, except for the daylight part of Saturday, leaped around the dining-room table in a gauze tunic and chamois slippers à la Isadora Duncan, or played a rented violin in the bathroom while Clara stood outside in her Indian blanket bathrobe, waiting to get in. Mildred had also become professionally acquainted with show business, though in a less direct way. She was going to Hunter in the day for her first two years, but she also had a part-time job with a new officer of the synagogue, a dentist with an office across the street from the back entrance of Madison Square Garden, where depending on the season, she helped him fill the teeth of midgets, giants, tattooed ladies, heavy middleweights, and broncobusters. My father loved the cowboys the best; as much as Florida these days, the Wild West attracted him. Yosel, of course (or "S. Joseph," as he now signed himself), needed spending money to take girls out on dates, and for him my father rented a tuxedo so that he could appear as an extra in a movie called *Moonlight and Pretzels*. Big Joe had gone back to Norfolk, unwed alas, but with great stories, so Cathrael sent up another son, Meyer Isaac, who had made the transition from Izzy to Easy, and whom my father got a job as an usher at the Strand Theater, where he saw George Arliss in *The Man Who Played God* for two months. Then came Easy's younger brother, Oscar Brandeis, who briefly agreed to become a sandwich man for the Danceland Ballroom.

My father was very pleased that the three young men, his own and Cathrael's two, soon became such fast friends, cousins and brothers, going out to Coney Island for the rides and the boardwalk, walking through Central Park at night talking about life and assuring each other that times would soon improve. They were good boys, who could be depended on to fill out a minyan in a pinch, just as Big Joe in his day had gone around on his part-time job as a messenger for Western Union, saying as instructed, " 'The Actors Temple' needs men in the morning." Sam Rosh, also a decent sort, though a cousin of Easy's and Oscar's on Fredel's side, joined them, and in summer all four boys went to baseball games. But dark morose Oscar, who had a strange habit of suddenly crooning a popular song into a person's ear and then whistling the chorus, really didn't like New York. He didn't mind seeing Negroes perform at the benefits, or even hugging my father, he just didn't want to eat with them at the same lunch counters. After he went back to Norfolk, he kept sending my father original songs that he wanted some famous star to introduce, and also announced that he was now starring on his own radio program as "Oscar the Warbler."

A few times Cathrael himself came up north, bringing a crate of fresh eggs, green figs from his garden, the famous Fredel, a brocaded Chippendale chair for the new apartment, and a beautiful inlaid chess table for my father. The two of them fell silent over it, leaving off their talk about Roosevelt's New Deal, the darkening situation in Europe, and the happy fact that the match made between Cathrael's daughter Anna and Rabbi Lekhem's son Louis had culminated in one of the largest Jewish weddings in Norfolk history, featuring practically an entire parliament of rabbis, with Rabbi Lekhem and Rabbi Gordon and my father among others crowded upon the altar, and my mother and Julia and me in the front pew. (The trip down had had an all too familiar ring to my father, what with Julia and I jammed into the same upper berth, and my mother and he below, but this he didn't mention to his brother.) "Children, children," my father laughed when it was dinnertime and he and Cathrael had each had the satisfaction of winning two games, "you'll both get a chance to sit next to Uncle," pleased that though Julia and I were pinching and shoving each other as usual, this time it was only because we both adored this charming, stouter version of himself.

Sometimes another, different brother came over too. Hershel, grim-faced and ashen, whose voice barely rose above a whisper. ("Listen, Channele," my father said, "if somebody hit you over the head with a shovel, you wouldn't have much to shout about either.") Hard as it was to believe, Hershel was in America because of his involvement in a romantic love triangle. He had been making time with his brother Shlomo's girl in Russia, and Shlomo, like a fool, had rushed back to the old country, just when he was about to become a citizen, in order to break them up. Shlomo had stayed, and Hershel had come to America and married a red-haired woman also named Goldie, who more than made up for his silence, and whose glittering side teeth matched her name. All she seemed to want in life was for my father to get her a fox-trimmed coat wholesale. Nobody said anything about the oldest brother, Yankel, who it turned out had been absconding with money meant for the family in Europe. "So you also have a Fanny," Clara said with a certain grim satisfaction.

As with the acts at the benefits, the big question was where to put people. The new apartment on Fifty-first

Street, reached by a grilled elevator, had a shower, a refrigerator instead of an icebox, and a private telephone, but was hardly big enough for the rest of us, much less visitors, since there were only two little bedrooms. My father and mother slept in one, and Julia and Sarah and I in the second, Julia with a whole bed to herself because she was fat, and Sarah and I together in the other one because we were skinny, all three head to toe like sardines. ("Mama, Julia's putting her foot in my face!" "*Shah!*" "But she's older." "You're smarter.") Yossie, being a boy, slept in a tiny separate alcove off the living room together with a Philco radio console and two bookcases containing my father's Hebrew tomes and assorted jokebooks, and Mildred slept on a daybed in the dining room, where my father typed away at the big round table far into the night, working the carriage from right to left and smoking Turkish cigarettes which he held between thumb and forefinger as he squinted through the smoke at his Yiddish page. When a stray nephew stayed with us, or Zayde came for his month, Mildred got transferred to the living-room sofa and whoever it was landed on the dining-room couch.

"You should be nicer to him," Clara said one spring day when Zayde had gone out to air himself in Central Park, and my father was leafing through *A Guide for the Perplexed,* preparing for a sermon.

"Zayde? Why?"

"Because he's my father."

"Clara, he's never been a father to anyone. He was awful to you. How can you forget that?"

"He's a *sheyner man.* A beautiful man. He has all his own teeth. You should take him around more. Introduce

hour. I'm not going to see the show. I'm only going back-stage."

"What's backstage?" Mildred piped up, coming back to life and putting in her two cents' worth, as usual.

"Where they undress," my father said, wishing too late that he had bitten his tongue out first.

Zayde's rheumy eyes gleamed with sudden interest. He decided to get out before Clara took it into her mind that Zayde should come with him.

"So at least wrap up good," Clara said finally, glancing from one to the other and acknowledging defeat. She followed him to the door and handed him a muffler. To keep the peace he took it, and when he got outside shoved it into a side pocket of his velvet-collared chesterfield. Actually, the late October night was a bit chilly, but even if it hadn't been, she would have insisted he wrap up good. Once he had asked her sister, Sarah, if Clara had always been like this, hysterical, but Sarah, much younger, couldn't remember. "Clara is Clara," Sarah had laughed, with that jolly acceptance of human nature, though her own life with jealous Harry Pollack was far from an easy one. As usual, he wished more of Sarah could have gone into Clara besides the voluptuous figure and high coloring. But as it was, Clara was getting to look more like her father and less like her sister every day. Unnervingly so. Put a goatee on Clara and she and Moses would have been carbon copies of each other.

He said good evening to a few firemen lounging outside station house 54, sidestepped a derelict, and crossed Eighth Avenue, passing the Automat, the Edison Hotel, the Mansfield Theater, a couple of speakeasies and little Italian restaurants. And here was Broadway. He was rarely there at night, and as always the sudden sight of it

him. Why do you fix the cards so every time he plays casino with Chanie he loses?"

"Oh, Clara, you're being utterly ridiculous."

"I'm ugly and ridiculous?"

"Utterly," my father said. "I said *utterly*. You know, it wouldn't hurt if you learned a little English."

"Like Anita?"

"Anita's my secretary. Of course she knows English. She also knows Hebrew."

"Secretary," Clara said. "Hebrew."

"Clara, please—"

"I'm not educated but I know."

"Know what? What do you think—? Never mind. Just leave me in peace, please."

"I'll leave you, don't worry. I'll leave you and take the two children with me."

He held his head in both his hands.

Anita, of whom Clara was so feverishly suspicious, was a beautiful girl, it was true, in the Palestinian style, with a black bun, silver Bezalel earrings and a mezuza to match. She was also shy, and engaged to a young rabbinical student. He had been lucky to get her. "Secretary?" Mr. Meltzer cried, his hops and brews business gone bankrupt with the end of Prohibition. "Now you need a secretary?" But the new officers had been all for it, among them an amiable fight doctor to whom we all went for sprains and bruises, and a Tammany lawyer. Not only did Anita type and file, she also ran errands for Clara, who came over practically every morning to poke around or maybe filch a piece of merchandise meant for the Ladies Auxiliary rummage sale. In addition, Anita knew enough Hebrew to spell him in the beginning grades of the Talmud Torah so that he could concentrate on getting such *momzerim* as Seymour Katz ready for their bar mitzvahs. *"Boruch hu es adonoy ha m'vorach,"* he said in the schoolroom upstairs over and over again, while red-haired Seymour spat out Indian-nut shells on the teacher's desk. Since my father knew he already sounded like a broken record, sometimes he wondered if he shouldn't make a real one in the penny arcade for Seymour to take home and study from, spitting out his nutshells in his own house.

"Anita," he said, descending from one of these sessions and leafing through the files after Clara had departed with a pair of donated potholders, "send a cable to Sophie Tucker in London. Tell her she has yahrzeit for her mother on the second day of Iyar, which corresponds to the evening of May thirtieth. Oh, and call Red at the Latin Quarter and tell him he can't get married on June tenth because that's between Pesach and Shevuoth. Tell him any date after the thirteenth will be fine. . . . Anyone call?"

"Your brother-in-law Alex. He wants free tickets for *Waiting for Lefty.*"

"Tell him it isn't playing anymore."

"Also Miss Bohan. She wants to know if you'll hand out the medal for journalism again this year."

"Again journalism?" my father said, wondering if she would ever break down and let him have the benediction or invocation, though he knew the priest from St. Malachy's had long had them both sewn up. Maybe she was afraid he would spring a wholesale conversion on her.

"Who's winning it this year?"

"Julia."

Julia? An interesting surprise. She was shaping up, in a manner of speaking, though she still cried whenever Clara made her wear a corset, and had found friends in the neighborhood: Shetawnwy Whitefeather, a full-blooded Indian, and also Isabella Zaphinopoulos, the daughter of the Greek Orthodox priest. Still, journalism? He hadn't realized that any of his children but Yosel were gifted in that direction.

"Did anyone else call?"

"Ely Kapetsky."

"What did *he* want?" my father said.

"He wouldn't tell me. He said it was private and personal. He's coming in about one."

"Okay," my father said. He looked at his watch. "Why don't you go get yourself some lunch?"

"But, Rabbi, I brought myself a cheese sandwich from home."

"It's okay. Take a little walk while you're at it. It's a beautiful day. Go over to Poliacoff's. Tell him I said it's on the house."

"All right, Rabbi. Thank you. Can I bring you anything?"

"I also have a cheese sandwich. Maybe you can bring me some coffee."

Ely Kapetsky came promptly, a small dark embittered young man with an unpleasant smile.

"What is it, Ely?" my father said, beckoning him to Anita's vacated chair on the other side of the desk. "What can I do for you?"

"It's my wife."

"Is she sick again? I'll go to see her."

"She's always sick."

"Well, with a weak heart. And two young children. It's not easy for her, you know, Ely."

"It's not easy for me, either."

"Of course not, that's understood."

"I'm only thirty years old," Ely said. "It's not too late to start over."

"It's never too late to start over. We do it every year on Rosh Hashanah, not to mention all the days in between. As the sages tell us—"

"I want a divorce."

"A divorce?" my father said. "Are you trying to kill her?"

"I have my own life to consider."

"Of course you do. Of course you do. But what kind of life? She's a good woman. She's doing her best."

"It's not good enough," Ely said. "I didn't know she was a sick woman when I married her. I want to be free."

"Free? I'll tell you a story," my father said, smiling. "A young man once said to an old man, 'What is life's heaviest burden?' And the old man said, 'To have nothing to carry.'"

"Give me a divorce," Ely said.

"All right," my father agreed, brisk and businesslike. "And on what grounds?"

"I know the Jewish law. I don't need any grounds. I'm a man."

"You're a man, Ely? You don't even know the first thing about it. Do me a favor. Forget about this divorce business for a while. Go home and start learning how to be a *mentsh*."

"Well, maybe you're right," Ely said, getting up and smiling slyly. "Maybe I don't need a divorce, after all."

"Good."

"I mean, *you* performed my wedding ceremony, didn't you? So maybe I was never even married."

My father closed his eyes until the echo of Ely's footsteps had died away. Better, far better, to have the Irish children run up and taunt him, than suffer a visit from that blackbird of misery.

As it happened, he could not brood on the matter for long, or on the bad taste Ely had left in his mouth, so bad it poisoned his cheese sandwich, even when washed down with Anita's coffee. There was too much else on his mind. Zayde had had a stroke—during his stay with Big Sarah, otherwise Clara would have held him to blame—and he was now trying to get him admitted to the Home of Old Israel. A terrible fate, to end one's days in an old age home, but there was no other way. And curiously, Clara didn't seem to mind. In fact, her personal dream for him and her was for both of them to retire to an old age home as soon as possible. She seemed to think it would be the best way to get away from the children. Maybe it would be a good idea to send Clara and the two youngest to the mountains for a month. He could only afford a *cochaleyn*—which meant that Clara would have to cook, sharing a stove with several other families—and really couldn't afford even that, but at least she would relax a bit, breathe some fresh air, pick and fuss with the leaves and flowers she so loved. Also, there was now every week his new radio program to prepare for, "The Schlossman Court of Arbitration" on WEVD, on which he had become a judge, adjudicating on such matters as whether a man whose leg had been amputated, which required a burial plot of its own, could expect his lodge to provide him with another plot when the rest of him died. Answer: definitely. Or, what a converted *shikse* could do to earn the respect of her Jewish mother-in-law. Answer: not much. "Channele didn't want to hear you!" Clara cried one night. "She wanted to listen to Eddie Cantor." My father looked at me in surprise.

On his Hebrew typewriter he was also writing a weekly column for the *Tag*, offering such opinions as "The greatness of Jews is that they are a nation of dreamers." And "Every tyrant who has tried to destroy the eternal Jewish people has failed. And so will Hitler. He must." A photograph of him appeared in the *World-Telegram*. Along with other rabbis from the Knesset Harabonim, of which he was secretary, he was seated at a long table set with a black cloth and black candles. Their revered leader, Rabbi Wolf Margolies, in his gabardine and bifurcated white beard, sat in the middle. They had declared a *cheyrim*, a boycott on all German goods. . . . "What is it this time, Clara?" he said, looking up. "The baby called Dominick, Hitler." "Why?" "He was hitting a carp over the head for the gefilte fish." "She's high-strung. We know that." . . . The correspondence with Russia became frantic. Shlomo, the twin sisters and their husbands, the mother—had they been receiving any money? Could they get out?

And every day my father walked what was becoming his beat, the length and breadth of Forty-seventh Street from Tenth Avenue all the way over to the jewelers off Fifth— pleading for funds, for goods, for donations, money for the poor, for the victims of Hitler, for the pioneers in Palestine—now known to every ticket taker, store owner, and theater manager in the area, and ultimately winding up with a connection for practically everything: insurance, ladies and gents clothing, wines and liquors, funeral chapel limousines, wholesale Persian-lamb coats, cocktail rings, kosher delicatessen, upholstering, carpentry, house painting, movie passes, railroad passes, doctors, dentists, a tailor who turned double-breasted tuxedos into single-breasted tuxedos and vice versa. "Daddy," I said one day, after we had arranged for Hershel's Goldie's cloth coat with the fox collar, "do only Gentiles buy retail?" "*Oy, mein kind.*"

Ordinarily, my father would have looked forward to performing Red Baxter's wedding. It had been a pleasure over the years to watch Red's progress from a shy, freckle-faced chorus boy to a mature, auburn-haired comedian known nationwide. In Ella Trent, herself a gifted tap dancer, Red had found a lovely girl. And of course, my father had already married many other people in show business. Among them, Harry Ritz of the Ritz Brothers, at the synagogue, all three mugging wildly; Judge Shalleck to the torch singer Lillian Roth, at the Savoy Plaza; Fred Finklehoff to Ella Logan, whom my father had converted, impressing on her the duties of a good Jewish wife, while admiring her cute little pug nose. But with weddings at home in the living room, "the rabbi's study," as it became known on such occasions, Clara usually got hysterical. Every time a guest put out a cigarette in a snake plant or the goldfish bowl, her greenish eyes popped and she made strangled noises. That plus the fact that today Sarah and Mildred were away at work and Yosel at college, which left Julia and me to hold the poles of his red-velvet portable wedding canopy. We had sworn to be good, and he had been hoping to see some sign of this famous goodness by the time the wedding began, but we had been engaged in our usual dialogue since three in the afternoon and showed no signs of an intermission.

Channele: Eddie Cantor never called *you* "little lady" when we went backstage at his radio show. He said it to me.

Julia: Oh, yeah? Well, I have witnesses.

C.: Yeah? Well, yesterday Milton Berle tipped his hat to me.

J.: He tipped his hat to Mama.

C.: Where was Mama?

J.: Right behind you.

Pause.

C.: Anyway, Daddy's going to get Bill Robinson to give me tap dancing lessons. I'm practically the same age as Shirley Temple.

J.: Ha, ha.

Another pause. The house was filling up. Red, hidden away in Yossie's sleeping alcove, alias "the rabbi's library," peered nervously into the living room where the guests had assembled, among them his prospective in-laws. "Keep it down to six or seven minutes, Rab," he whispered. "This is a tough audience." "I've played to tougher," my father assured him, hearing in the distance: "You only had double pneumonia. I had an operation." To which Julia responded: "You think you're so smart."

"Kinder," my father said, emerging into the center of the room with Red trailing behind him, and smiling a smile he did not exactly feel. He positioned the bridal pair, and with Julia and me holding opposite poles of the portable *chupa*, my arm upraised as far as it would go, and two of Red's friends holding the other poles, he com-

menced the ceremony. "*Adir eloheynu. Simen tov u ma-zel tov. Chasan boruch hu. Cala borucha v'na'a. . . .* Blessed is the bridegroom, blessed and beautiful is the bride." He paused. This was the place where he always gave a little speech, a speech which for the sake of all concerned he had decided to make even littler.

"Friends, my dear friends, we are gathered here this afternoon to see united in marriage two distinguished members of the theatrical community, Red Baxter and Ella Trent. Distinguished not only by their God-given gifts and their talents, but by the joy they give to others, and the joy which in their love they give to each other. Distinguished by their devotion to their beloved parents, and to the ideals of our Jewish faith. How do I know this? I know this because I first met Red when he came to my synagogue to say kaddish for his father. It was right after a matinee, and I . . ."

Julia and I were making cockeyes at each other. He stopped to glare at us. "But—my friends—what is marriage? A true Jewish marriage? Is it the mere union of two young people who have fallen in love? A mere infatuation? Or is it something deeper, something finer? 'I have never called my wife, my wife,' said Rabbi Jose, one of our great sages, 'I have called her my house.' And what did he mean by that?" The progeny of his own Jewish marriage were now sticking out their tongues at each other under the *chupa* and waggling their fingers in their ears. He would deal with them later, oh, would he deal with them later. Meanwhile, with a short peremptory cough, he answered his own rhetorical question as succinctly as possible, and blessed the goblet of wine for the bridal pair to sip from.

"And now, do you Israel Tannenbaum, of your own free

{ 125 }

will and accord take Esther Shapiro to be your wife? And do you promise to love, honor, and cherish her all the days of her life?" Red said, "I do" in a barely audible voice, and so when her turn came did Ella, despite their theatrical training.

"Now, Red, put this ring on her finger"—I was about to speak up, but my father got there first—"no, the forefinger of her right hand, you can change it after . . . and repeat after me, '*Harey at—m'kudeshes—li—b'tabaas—moshe v' yisroel.* Behold—thou art consecrated unto me—with this ring—in accordance with the law—of Moses—and of Israel.' Good. You're a quick study, Red."

In rapid Hebrew he read the *kesubah*, the marriage contract, and then more slowly in English: "On this, the twenty-second day of June 1936, corresponding to the Hebrew date, the twentieth day of Sivan, 5696, the said bridegroom plighted his troth unto his wife, saying . . ." He gave them the goblet of wine to sip from again, praised God who had created the universe, and God who had created man, and with real tears of joy in his eyes (such a beautiful couple) invoked His blessings on the happy pair. And then, in a louder, triumphant voice, he said: "I now pronounce you man and wife, according to the laws of Moses and of Israel, and the state of New York. . . . Step on the glass, Red. Wonderful. And now you may kiss the bride."

At the breaking of the shot glass, which he bought by the dozen at Woolworth's and which Clara had wrapped in newspaper—once she had wrapped up a saltshaker, which the groom had been unable to break—Clara poked her head into the living room, eyes wide, making frantic gestures, as if she had just truly been present at the destruction of the Temple. Amid cries of "*Mazel tov!*" my father sent Julia and me off to fold and put away the portable canopy, leaving no doubt that he would be heard from later.

"Clara," he said, having shaken hands and smiled as he made his way through the room. "What is it with this family? So I'll buy you another snake plant. Can't you see that I—?"

"What are you talking?" she cried. "Zayde had another stroke. Zayde died!"

"Killed him? Sure I killed him," my father said grimly, addressing himself to Big Sarah as the only normal one among Clara's many relatives who had laid siege to his dining room in their stockinged feet for seven long days. "I paid for the Home of Old Israel, didn't I? I officiated at his funeral and got a free plot from the shul besides, didn't I? Isn't that tantamount to murder?"

"Take it easy, Beril," Big Sarah said, cheerfully nibbling at some glazed fruit, brought as a shiva offering by one of the balabatim. "You know Clara, she likes to fly off the handle. She doesn't mean anything by it."

My mother, who had started off by not speaking to her husband and was now not speaking to her sister either, sniffed bitterly.

"Aha! But in a capitalist society there are all different degrees of murder," her brother Alex said, immediately seconded by his wife and fellow party member, Reena, whose eyeglasses looked like the bottoms of Coke bottles. "There is first of all the murder of the working classes by the bosses."

"Bosses," echoed another brother Max, a relative latecomer to America, who had been down in Norfolk minding Moses' old grocery store, and was also a Communist. (Did they grow on trees in this family?) "Believe me, Beril, comes the revolution—"

"I know," my father said, wistfully recalling the comedian Willie Howard, "we'll *all* eat strawberries and cream."

"Chana," my mother said. "Tell Papa he didn't have any lunch yet."

"Mama says you didn't have any lunch yet."

"I have to call the shul first. Then I'll have something."

"He has to call the shul first. Then he'll have something."

"A wonderful son-in-law," my mother said. "For his balabatim he doesn't eat, he doesn't sleep, he writes *droshes*, but to play casino with his father-in-law for a few minutes . . ."

"Come on, Clara," Big Sarah said. "Zayde wasn't a father to anybody, much less a father-in-law. We have to face that nobody liked him." Nodding, Max helped himself to another piece of fruit from the steamer basket sent by Mr. Alter. Hymie and his Goldie, and Alex and Reena did likewise. It was the fourth steamer basket they had gone through, starting first with Sophie Tucker's, which had appealed to Hymie immediately. A perennially worried Harry Pollack shook his head.

My father went into the living room and closed the glass French doors before he dialed the synagogue number and got Anita on the phone. "Anything new? I should be back for *mincha* if this crew ever clears out."

"Ed Sullivan has a very nice mention of you in 'Talk of the Town.' Listen, 'Broadwayites are saying that Rabbi Birstein of the Actors Temple is the one Broadway personality who never changes his act. The little rabbi's role

"Fine," my mother said. "Why shouldn't they be fine? They're in high school."

"She has such a nice figure, Sarah."

"A nice figure isn't everything. You have to have *mazel*."

"And Yosel? Is he still handsome? I bet he has a lot of girl friends."

"He's not only handsome. He goes to NYU."

"Doesn't NYU cost a lot of money?" Hymie asked.

"Come, Clara."

My mother buttoned me up in my leggings, while Julia struggled into her red chinchilla coat and matching hat with pompons, fetching her corkscrew curls out from under her collar. Hymie tried again.

"You know, Beril, I bet one word from you—"

"Listen, Hymie," my father said, putting on his chesterfield, the signal for everybody to get up and accompany us to the door. "At the benefits, the people who used to sing 'Give My Regards to Broadway,' are now singing 'Brother, Can You Spare a Dime?' "

Harry Pollack's cheeks suddenly reddened with embarrassment. He drew my father aside. "Listen, Beril—"

My father nodded and waved a hand. "Forget it."

"I assure you that as soon as I—"

"Don't worry about it."

"Give Big Sarah a kiss," my mother said.

I did.

"I wish you were my mommy," I said.

"*Oy, a broch*," Big Sarah said.

"I didn't teach her anything. She likes her aunt."

sheviks and schnorrers in his dining room. But Clara, though she refused to speak to him herself, would grow suspicious of any prolonged conversation with someone else. As he opened the French doors again, the word *Italiener* hung in the air, and he somehow understood that Clara's sister Fanny was sitting shiva alone in her apartment.

"I'll eat something now," he said.

Clara bustled off into the kitchen.

"Channele, you don't look very well," he remarked, reaching out a hand to touch my forehead. "Maybe I should try your fever."

"I'm fine," I said, wriggling out from under.

"What do you want? She hasn't had any air all week," Big Sarah said.

"I know. But Clara wanted her to stay home from school in Zayde's honor."

"So why not Julia too?"

"Because there was no earthly reason for either of them to stay home."

"No early reason," my mother said bitterly, returning. "Tell Papa I put cabbage soup with *flanken* on the table."

"Daddy, there's cabbage soup with *flanken* on the table."

"Thank you. I heard her."

"Also rye bread."

"Also rye bread."

"I don't need the complete menu," my father said.

"So next year at this time, we'll have to put up a stone," Harry Pollack said. "And where will we get the money?"

"Beril will find a way," Big Sarah said. "It doesn't have to be big."

"Money is no objection," Max said.

{ 130 }

"Channele, tell your uncle he's here to sit shiva, not to bore from within."

"Daddy says—"

"Never mind," my father said, starting off for the kitchen. He paused and gave me another dubious look. "Channele, I still don't like the way you look. You have dark circles under your eyes."

"I always have dark circles under my eyes."

"Nevertheless, you have school again tomorrow. I want you to get a good night's sleep tonight."

"Oh, I don't sleep anymore."

"Why not?"

"Julia said dying was going to sleep and never waking up."

"Brilliant," my father said, "absolutely brilliant. I'd like to know where she got that from."

My mother looked away casually, as if she hadn't heard, and cracked a nut with a nutcracker.

"And the other girls?" Big Sarah said. "I hardly saw them around all week."

"Dixie's going out with a real aviator," I said. "His name is Ace and he wears a white scarf around his neck."

"An aviator *af mayn kop*," my mother began with gusto, and my father abandoned a possible philosophical discourse on death to go and eat his cabbage soup.

For the first time since my father had traveled on the road, he was going to be living the life of a bachelor. During the month that my mother and Julia and I were to be at the *cochaleyn*, Sarah and Mildred would be spending their two-week vacations at Camp Tamiment in the Poconos. Sarah was no longer Dixie. She had tired of her

southern accent; it was hard to sustain and it got her no-
where. For reasons she didn't want to talk about, Ace was
suddenly no longer her boyfriend. My father, much as he
hated to agree with Clara on these matters, was just as
glad she had broken off with him. All flash and no sub-
stance. He had worried every time they drove off in the
young man's red convertible, but it was hard to tell a girl,
especially one who worked so hard, not to have a good
time. Ace had been briefly supplanted by Walter, a flo-
rist, who had presented my mother with a gardenia plant.
But far from pleasing her, the plant only made her nervous. She could not seem to adapt to gardenias growing
live in a little green bush instead of lying yellowish and
waxen in a corsage with a silver ribbon. In fact, the plant
had made everyone a little uneasy, and once when no one
was around and my father leaned over to smell it, the
word *Everglades* had flashed through his mind.

When the last gardenia fell off, Sarah had got rid of
Walter and changed her name, this time working from
Soreh to Sorkeh to Sookie. Which was all right, except
that she got Mildred mixed up in it too, and made her call
herself Mookie. Sookie and Mookie. Again all right, but
on top of that they were supposed to dress themselves up
like twins, which not only meant spending every last
penny of their salaries on clothes, instead of saving up for
their marriages as Clara wanted them to do, but put
Mildred at a distinct disadvantage. Mildred, unlike Sarah,
was neither lithe nor slender, but stocky and patient. In
their matching navy blue jumpers and Breton hats with
the elastic under their chins, Sarah looked like a cute little
schoolgirl and Mildred like an abandoned orphan. What
she would do at a place like Camp Tamiment he didn't
know. Her real interest was art, which she had been

majoring in at Hunter College, and she could sit for hours at the dining-room table sketching in charcoal, frowning and erasing, the only time she kept quiet, while her best friend Evelyn, whose mother was a widow, sat and watched her silently. Still, the Camp Tamiment project was one of which Clara approved. They would never find husbands in Hell's Kitchen, she insisted, never mind Times Square. And twins did run in his family.

As a favor to Clara, who was speaking to him again, he took Julia and me off her hands on the day she was packing for the country, a Herculean task involving pots and bedding, by treating us to a two-pound brown paper bag of cherries and a Fifth Avenue bus ride. It was a hot sunny day. We boarded the green double-decker in front of a jewelry store at Forty-seventh and Fifth, scrambling right up the stairs to the top, which was marvelously open to the sky. The conductor came by with his change machine, and my father importantly put three dimes in the slots. A dime for a bus ride! Already he could see that we were thrilled. Never mind the sun beating down on our heads, and the hot wicker seats imprinting themselves on our bare legs. We had been to the theater many times over, and to the movies, and Bear Mountain, but we had never been on a Fifth Avenue bus before. He sat in the middle, having established that Julia would sit next to the outside railing going downtown, and I next to the outside railing going uptown. Julia didn't know that the downtown part of the ride was shorter, but he would deal with that when and if it came up. Besides, she liked cherries.

As we rode past them, he pointed out the fancy, expensive department stores, Lord and Taylor, W. and J. Sloane, B. Altman, though none so fine to his mind as Marshall Field in Chicago. There was also the Forty-second Street Library with its two big gray stone lions, where Yosel spent so much of his time. He had heard there was even a Yiddish room with Yiddish books in it. Then past the fine crystal and china in the wholesale windows of the Twenties and on down toward Greenwich Village. At the beautiful carved stone arch in Washington Square the bus stopped, and Julia and I set up our usual howl, thinking it was all over. But my father quieted us with an upraised hand and a knowing smile. When the conductor came around again, my father let me and Julia put our own dimes in the slots, making a grand total of sixty cents coming and going. Julia and I changed places, and we started back up Fifth Avenue, but on the other side. He took off his panama hat, mopped his brow with a clean white handkerchief, and quickly covered his head again. Julia and I were getting hot and restless, and had begun to spit cherry pits down on the passersby. He tried to ignore us and enjoy the ride.

"*Kinder*, please," he said, when that failed. "What have you got against pedestrians? Soon you'll be in the country."

"I hate the country," I said.

"You were never *in* the country," Julia said.

"If it's like Central Park, I hate it," I said. "I want to stay with Daddy."

"Your mother would miss you," my father said.

"Mama hates me. She only likes Julia."

"Channele, don't be foolish. I expect more of you than that."

For a while Julia and I spat down our cherry pits in sullen silence. The bus started across Fifty-seventh Street, and my father pointed out Carnegie Hall, where all the great musicians of the world gave concerts. The renowned cantor, Yossele Rosenblatt, had also performed there. "We're not so far from home, you know," he said, "it just feels far. That's the advantage of travel."

"Won't you be lonesome?" I said, as we started up Broadway past the Colonial, once a vaudeville house, but now showing Victor McLaglen in *The Informer*.

"Lonesome? Why should I be lonesome? Yosel will be home at night."

Yosel, who knew nothing about food, was to be a food checker on the Albany Night Line over the summer. Sam Rosoff, the subway builder, who now also came to shul, had got him the job.

"Sookie and Mookie got new bathing suits," I said.

"Two-piece," Julia added. "Mama said—"

"They should wear them in good health," my father finished for her quickly.

The bus was now going across Seventy-second Street, and then up Riverside Drive. Lonesome. No, it wouldn't be much of a problem. He could always make himself an egg in the evening, butter a roll. Also, Mrs. Alter was eager to feed him, and so was Mrs. Goldman, though for the sake of his weak stomach he did not think he would take them up on it. And there was always Poliacoff's "The Aristocrat of Kosher Cooking" over on Forty-fifth and Broadway next to The Lobster, though it meant being visited at the table by the founder, whose portrait hung on the wall, and whose bulging eyes and black walrus mustache were not exactly conducive to a hearty appetite. The sun was beating down hard. He pointed out New Jersey to the left, and the trees of the Palisades, but Julia and I were flushed and drowsy and inattentive. The river sparkled. He thought of how behind him it opened up into the harbor, and of Ellis Island, and the Statue of Liberty. On the right were the big apartment houses and elegant mansions where the rich Jews such as the Schwabs lived. Riverside Drive was the top of the world and he was on top of Riverside Drive. No, he did not think he would be lonesome.

Two weeks later, Sarah came back from Camp Tamiment, still Sookie but otherwise defeated.

"Don't cry, *mein kind*," my father said to her with a certain male helplessness. "It's not worth crying over."

"Oh, Papa, you don't understand," Sarah said. "I know nobody's ever going to love me."

"What are you saying? Channele has already sent you nine picture postcards."

"That's not what I'm talking about."

"I know it," my father sighed, leaning back in the kitchen chair. She buttered him a piece of pumpernickel and he thoughtfully bit off a piece, sipping at his coffee. It was night. Usually, Sarah practiced her violin in the bathroom at this hour, but now that she was back from Camp Tamiment, she was too depressed and listless. When Mildred said she no longer wanted to dress up as twins, Sarah had not bothered to argue the matter. He did not know what went on in such "adult" camps, but he could imagine. Was the old way of fixing up a match, a *shidach*, more insulting to the human spirit than parading around in a two-piece bathing suit? It was hard to tell.

"Sarah," he said, "it's *nice* to kiss a boy. It's nice when he kisses you back. It makes you feel good. And if he doesn't see you in the city, that's not so terrible either."

"It's this eye," she said bitterly. "It makes me ugly. She's right about my needing an operation."

"What are you talking about? Nobody even notices it."

"I do."

"Well, if you really feel that way, then you should have it fixed."

"How? With what? It's so expensive. I don't give you anything at home, and I've tried to save up from my salary, but—"

"We'll find a way," my father said.

"Oh, Papa, you'll never climb out of debt as it is."

Which certainly on the surface seemed true. Only recently, Channele had asked if Morris Plan was a friend of his. "We'll find a way," my father said.

Sarah nodded and blew her nose. She looked very tired and much too thin in her yellow seersucker bathrobe, but she made herself sip a little coffee.

"Look, Sarah," he said, "I know your life isn't an easy one. You work hard all day, and then when you come home—"

"She makes us hot lunches. That's nice of her."

"She believes in food, like Maimonides. He says the Mishna begins with the dietary laws because food is the first essential to living." My father sighed. "Of course, he goes on to other essentials."

"Do you believe in a *basherte*?" Sarah said. "That there's one person who's destined for you?"

"Some people do."

"But then you don't have to look for him. He finds *you*."

"I think it takes a little of both," my father said. "As in everything else."

"What did my mother look like?" Sarah said.

"Your mother? Well, she was thin, like you. She—you have the picture. You have the ring with the green stone."

"You can't tell much. She's wearing glasses."

"That's true," my father said.

"Was she beautiful?"

"She was beautiful," my father said.

Unfortunately, my vacation didn't seem to have done any more for me than for my sisters. Pale as ever, once I too was back from the country, I either sat moping downstairs on the stoop, or upstairs at the dining-room table. "Summer *stinks*," my father found me writing in my diary one August day when he came home from shul for lunch. It wasn't even a regular diary, but a brown pasteboard memo book that the Riverside Memorial Chapel had once sent to him and that he had given to me. "It is the minister's duty, when the occasion requires," the printed message inside read, "to recommend an undertaker who will comply with all the ethics of the profession. In such a case you may have full confidence in Riverside service." In the back, there were places for the names of the deceased.

"You should be outside playing," my father said.

"I don't have anybody to play with."

"Where's Tippy Klein?" he asked, referring to the kosher-butcher's daughter.

"I don't know and I don't care."

"What can you do?" my mother said, turning from the window where she was airing herself. "She's too smart for the other children." Adding, as if it were an affliction, "She has your head."

Yawning listlessly, I pushed aside my diary, and started to fool around with a ball of foil from discarded cigarette packages that I had been saving for the Spanish Loyalists. Tiring of that, I picked up a couple of paper dolls to marry. My father had to admit that I had the ceremony down pat, but that wasn't the point.

"Come, Channele," he said, thinking a moment. "We're going to a ball game."

"A ball game?"

"Certainly. Why not?"

"Beril, what are you talking? It's Friday!"

"It's also Ladies Day. Come."

My mother made us have some schav with a boiled potato and sour cream, and then we set out for the Polo Grounds on the Eighth Avenue subway. At the beginning of the season, my father explained as we rattled uptown, he had acquired a pass for all the Yankee and Giant home games. Naturally, he could have had a pass for Ebbets Field too, but who needed it?

"Yes, but, Daddy, do you know anything about baseball?"

"Certainly. I went with Sam Rosh when you were in the *cochaleyn*. I've studied."

"Who's playing?"

"The Giants and the Cubs," my father said, shaking his head with friendly exasperation. "But that's not the point. The point is that for twenty-five cents apiece for federal tax we can sit in the sunshine for a few hours and get some fresh air."

"Fresh air?"

At the stadium, alive with crowds and pennants, he put me on the Ladies line and then went to stand on the Press line along with the other priests and rabbis. As instructed, I waited for him inside the shadowy lower grandstand where he bought a scorecard, and then we climbed to the sunny upper tier, making our way around to Section 33, right behind third base. Some of the group already assembled there turned around to greet him. "Hi, Rab," Ted Lewis said, "I thought you were a Yankee fan." "It's a game. I'm here on account of the kid," my father said, introducing me to Jesse Block of Block and Sully, and Johnny Broderick, the famous detective, who sat there smiling, though there was the very evident bulge of a holster under his jacket. "Honey. Now that's a pretty name for a pretty little girl." I already knew Sam Dody of Lewis and Dody, also known as The Harmony Boys, now retired, who hung around the shul like an extra shammos.

"Channele, pay attention," my father said, as I wistfully turned to watch the vendors walking up and down with their unkosher hot dogs. He bought himself a Coke, me a bag of peanuts and an orange soda, and jotted down the lineup on his scorecard, showing me how it was done. "1, Carl Hubbell, pitching, we're lucky . . . 2, Hank Danning, catching, he's Jewish, you know . . . 9, Mel Ott, right field, what a hitter. . . ." The Cubs he gave short shrift. Nothing from Chicago attracted him.

Since we were in an exposed section, the sun beat down on us, though not as hard as on the poor people in the bleachers, but the grass smelled fresh and wet. Fat umpires in their blue uniforms ran around the bases as excitedly as the players. Then there would be a lull, and people would lean back and crack jokes or have a little refreshment. "Fielder's choice!" Ted Lewis cried after one play. "Fielder's choice," my father repeated solemnly, showing me how to mark down an "x" in the little box. "Sacrifice!" "Sacrifice." A double play was more complicated but more thrilling. Then Carl Hubbell was on the mound and it was 3 and 2 against Demaree, and my father leaped to his feet yelling, "Come on, strike him out, you *goslin*, strike him out!" "*Momzer! Momzer!*" I cried, leaping up with him. "Channele, sit down," my father said, subsiding. "But, Daddy, you—" Ignoring me, he cast a wary eye at the scoreboard for his Yankees, who were not doing too well in Boston, and then as the game proceeded kept looking up at the sun and at his watch. The days were growing noticeably shorter. At the top half of the seventh inning a few fans stood up, though not in Section 33, and he quickly put a restraining hand on my arm. "Channele," he said firmly, "for the home team you stretch before the *bottom* of the seventh."

While the players changed sides, Sam Dody decided to teach me one of his old routines. "Come on, Honey, try it. . . . *Hello, hello, hello*—repeat—*hello, hello, hello*—fish don't perspire—*hello, hello, hello*. . . . Not bad. . . . Try the 'cheery-bob-chick' again. Hm. . . . Well, how about this one? *The Red Sox were playing the White Sox, but the Red Sox were wearing blue sox and the White Sox . . .*"

Sam shook his head. "Frankly, Rab, she just hasn't got the stuff." My father shrugged philosophically. It was exactly what the tap dancing teacher had said about me when he gave my father his deposit back. In this case, which had to do with words rather than rhythm, he was not altogether convinced. Sam was now in insurance and had been away from show business a long time except for memories of past glories. He had never even held it against Sam that once when he and the shammos were robbed of a couple of suits and umbrellas they kept in the office, it turned out that they were only insured against the theft of Torahs.

By the bottom half of the ninth, I had had two orange sodas, another bag of peanuts, and had done a whole inning by myself on the scorecard, though under the strictest supervision. In Boston the Yankees had narrowed the lead but still trailed by two runs. At the Polo Grounds we were faced with a tie game and Mel Ott had not come through with a home run, though my father had yelled himself hoarse. He looked more and more nervously at his watch and at the sun. Abruptly he stood up. "Come, Channele." "But, Daddy." "*Shah.*" "What a shame you have to leave now, Rabbi," Johnny Broderick said. "It's only a game," my father said, walking out backwards. In the lower grandstand, he popped his head in one more time, and shook it slowly. Then he rushed us back toward the subway, stiffening a little when a roar went up behind us. At the Fiftieth Street station, he waved me toward home like a coach, and sped on toward the synagogue. When Red asked him after services why he was so hoarse, he said maybe he had a little cold coming on. When Clara asked him the same question after kiddush, he glared and said nothing.

They were both reading the newspaper, my mother the *Forward*, holding it up to the light and mouthing the words pleasantly to herself, my father the *Daily News*. We also got the *Tag*, the *Morgen Journal*, the *Daily Mirror*, the *World-Telegram*, and the *Post*. Whatever Yiddish paper my mother was reading, and it was always a Yiddish paper, that paper always seemed to have read an English paper, since she invariably reported the news a day late, along with her discoveries of what famous people were Jewish. While they nodded and "tsk"ed, I sat at the dining-room table doing my homework, hating school worse than ever and making no bones about it. I hated sitting straight as a ramrod at my desk, hands clasped in front of me, not speaking except on command, and having to ask permission to go to the bathroom, which only the bad children ever did anyway, and knowing that Mrs. Sinsheimer held the notorious affair of the bloomers against me too, as if heredity were involved, and being asked repeatedly why I wouldn't put my name down for activities at Hartley House. "It's a Catholic settlement house," my father said, "and you're not a Catholic."

"Shirley Ackerman goes."

"She's not a Catholic, either."

"Nora O'Connor said I killed Christ."

"*Oy, mein kind,*" my father said, "tell her to look at the dates."

He sighed now and pointed disgustedly to a news photograph of Edward VIII, formerly the Prince of Wales. "In terrible times like these we need a world leader," he said to my mother. "And what do we have in England? A *peytsadek.*"

"What's a *pey-tsadek?*" I asked.

My two suddenly silent parents looked at each other.

"Well, it's a—a—" My father cleared his throat. "Now his father, George, had distinction. That was a king."

"Like Roosevelt?"

"This is a democracy, *mein kind.*"

"Then why isn't she voting?" I said accusingly.

"Mama? Mama never votes."

{ *143* }

"Why not? In a democracy, isn't it a privilege people fight and die for?"

"Yes, surely, but—"

We were now free to discuss the matter quite openly, since my mother had vanished into the bedroom, taking the *Forward* with her.

"Didn't our forefathers come here in search of religious and political freedom?"

"Our forefathers," my father said. "I suppose in a manner of speaking—"

"Daddy, you *know* what I mean. Anyhow, it's the first duty of every citizen to vote. And Mama's a citizen. So she has to vote. Especially for Roosevelt."

"Well, you have a point," my father said. "And of course Lehman— Channele, how old are you now?"

"Nine."

"I think you're a little overdeveloped politically." He shrugged. "Okay. Go ahead and try it. I'll tell you what. I'll take her to register. You get her to the polls."

"I should take her to the polls?"

"Why not? It's P.S. 17. You know everybody there, anyhow."

In October, he brought her home wan and shaken. In the next few weeks, whenever she seemed to waver, I loudly recited the Pledge of Allegiance, and the Preamble to the Constitution of the United States, hard words included, or sang a few choruses of "America the Beautiful." My father on the whole approved of my patriotism. Hadn't he worn a cutaway and striped pants for his naturalization? Nevertheless.

"Channele," he said, "maybe you should lay off a little

bit. 'Not by My might, but by My spirit,' says the Lord—
Zechariah.'"

"She's a citizen."

"I'm a citizen on Papa's papers," my mother said, narrowing her eyes triumphantly.

What bothered her, of course, was not the voting but the signing. Little levers on a machine, she could tackle, she was handy. But anything involving reading and writing she backed away from. The *Forward* she read holding it up to the light, mumbling and crooning the words to herself. When it came to the *Daily News*, she wet her thumb and forefinger and flicked to the pictures. Still, as I pointed out, if she had signed her name once at registration, she could do it again. All she had to do was copy her own signature.

"I already voted," she said as election day drew near.

"You didn't. You registered."

"And if I don't vote is what? One vote will make a difference?"

"If everybody thought the way you do," I said, "nobody would vote at all. Do you realize that?"

She smiled, as complacent and self-righteous in her flowered housedress as the Statue of Liberty.

"You know what you are? You're a disgrace to your country."

"Beril, what does she want from my life? What did I ever do to her?"

"She wants to be proud of you," my father said.

On election day, my father went to the polls early. "Drop by the shul when you and Mama are finished," he said. I watched him leave the house with a sense of poignancy and regret. Usually I went with him, the only day I ever entered the portals of P.S. 17 willingly, and voted the straight Democratic ticket on the little model voting machine while he went inside and cast his ballot secretly.

As soon as he left, my mother said she wasn't feeling well. When I said she looked fine, she koshered a piece of brisket in a bucket of salt water, and then washed the kitchen floor, getting down on her hands and knees and covering it with newspapers. After that she aired all the bedding on the windowsills, stopping to listen to a saxophonist in the yard. By the time she finished finding her garters, it was past three. I was in an agony of impatience, but she dressed slowly, in the blue dress she had worn for the High Holidays, and then took her time putting on her worn black sealskin coat, readjusting her three spit curls before she placed on top of her head a black felt pot with a veil that went over her eyes and nose. We walked the few blocks past the Tivoli and Stillman's Gym slowly and silently, my mother stopping at each corner to take a few breaths. P.S. 17 had been transformed, a hushed place for grown-ups. I led my mother to the end of the line for our district and stood beside her. She waited gravely for her turn, staring straight ahead through her nose veil, and shrinking before my eyes as she always did on public occasions. Click, click, went the levers, the huge handle thrust the green curtains aside, someone would step out, and we would all move forward another place. Out of the corner of my eye I could see my little voting machine on its table against the wall. But I stayed at my mother's side, pushing her forward by the elbow when the blowsy gray-haired lady in charge of the ledger looked up. Mrs. Kelly, an ordinary tenant in our building, but today a person of heart-stopping dignity.

"Name?" she said sharply.

I told her.

{146}

"Age?"

"Twenty-one plus," I answered quickly.

"Listen," Mrs. Kelly said, "you can give me the address too because we both know what it is, but that's as far as we go. Your mother has to sign."

"Who said she wouldn't?"

Mrs. Kelly gave me a sour look, and shoved the ledger forward, pointing to the proper line and handing my mother the pen.

My mother turned to me with a wavering smile, like a person about to go for an operation. "Tell me the first letter," she said.

"Mama, please. Just copy what you did last time."

"One letter is no crime."

"Mama, it's illegal." I looked pleadingly at Mrs. Kelly, who sighed and nodded. "Okay, the first letter is C. Now please take it from there."

My mother gave Mrs. Kelly a woman-to-woman smile. "Her father is also a nervouser," she confided pleasantly, and bent to scratch in her name, pausing lengthily between each letter. With a quick impatient tilt of her head, Mrs. Kelly indicated the open and empty polling booth. I watched my mother as if from a great distance, wincing when she caught the big handle in her hat, tried to restore her crumpled crown and veil, and then with a mighty push enclosed herself within the political mysteries inside. Released, I went over to my machine. Frankly, I liked the symbols of the other parties a lot better than the simple star—the adorable hammer and sickle, the tiny torch, the miniature eagle, the little hands clasped together. But, as always, I voted the straight Democratic ticket, nodding with satisfaction as each lever fell into place. "Roosevelt and Garner," I murmured to myself,

"Lehman, Bray, Tremaine, Bennett, Rippey," until I came to the end of the row, and stepped aside for the benefit of any interested bystanders. There were none. I looked toward the polling booth. My mother's feet were still planted firmly beneath the curtains. Obviously, it was going to take her longer than it had taken me. I had merely whipped through the ballot knowing I could vote again and again if I pleased, whereas for her it was a great moment, serious business. I undid my levers and pressed them down all over again, this time making myself count to five before each one. "Roosevelt and Garner," I whispered to myself, "one, two, three, four, five. . . . Lehman, one, two, three, four, five. . . . Streit!" I cried triumphantly, and wheeled around, expecting to find my mother at my elbow. But no, my mother's feet were as before, still visible beneath the curtain, short wide feet in black patent leather oxfords. Only they were now on tiptoe, calves straining at her shiny service-weight stockings. Was she trying to read the *amendments*? Down came the heels, and then up again.

By now, about eight or ten people had accumulated in front of the booth, eight or ten angry people who, like me, were staring transfixed at my mother's feet. "What the hell they got in there, a dwarf?" someone said. I turned back to my voting machine and closed my eyes, praying to God and to Tammany Hall to get us out of there. When I opened my eyes, my mother still hadn't materialized—I no longer expected her to—and I went back to my voting. "Roosevelt and Garner," I whispered listlessly, "and Lehman, and—" A strange man, a newcomer in a derby, stopped to pat my head.

"And what have we here?" he cried jovially. "A little Democrat! And what's your name, little girlie?"

I couldn't decide whether to say "Anna" because we were in P.S. 17, or "Honey" because it was a holiday. I gave him a desperately bright smile, and he patted me again and said my mother must be very proud of me and went to take his place on the line. In a minute he was asking the man in front of him what was going on, and in another minute had joined in the general demand to get her out of there with a crowbar. I turned back to my machine, for the first time in my life sick and tired of voting the straight Democratic ticket. Should I try the American Labor party for a change? How long had she been there anyway? Wasn't there some law about how long you could take? What if somebody called the police, who were only two doors away? Just then there was a big thump and a general sigh of relief. My mother emerged from between the green curtains and reached out a hand for my shoulder. As we left the school, the democratic process picked up again behind us, and our line moved briskly forward. Outside, I took a deep breath at the first No Electioneering sign. It was good to be free of that awful place until tomorrow. My mother, hand still on my shoulder, was peculiarly silent. As we crossed the outer courtyard, I was waiting for her to tell me I was right, that there was nothing to it, that she was proud to be an American. But she was looking up at the sky with eyes full of puzzlement.

"Well," I said cheerfully, as we went down the stone stairs, "aren't you glad you did it? Won't you be proud tonight when the returns come in?"

"What?"

"I said won't you be— hey, where are you going? Daddy said to drop by the shul."

But she shook her head and kept on going east, toward Eighth Avenue. In front of Professor Mazocchi's Spaghetti

Parlor, she stopped short and gave me a terrible smile, then thrust her arm through mine as if we had suddenly become friends, which was scary.

"Tootsie—" she said, regarding me through her nose veil.

Tootsie?

"Toots-ele, you could keep a secret if I asked you in a nice way?"

"What kind of a secret?" I said darkly.

She abandoned the smile and sighed from the heart. "Don't tell Papa," she said dismally. "But I think I voted for Landon."

All through the next days, reading about the landslide in the newspapers and looking at maps which showed every state in the union white except for Maine and Vermont, which were black, I imagined I saw a tiny black fleck in a corner of New York, which was my mother's solitary vote for Landon. But I kept her secret, which was alas also mine, and my father didn't notice that anything was wrong. He was now too preoccupied with the new benefit, which was almost upon him, riffling through his tickets, selling ads for the journal, enlisting Yossie's help to make sure his message was written in good English. That year, in spite of all his worrying, it turned out to be a great success, featuring Bert Lahr in his plaid lumber jacket, bellowing, "Woodsman, spare that tree!" And Willie Howard as Professor Marquette, giving his French course in "ten easy lessons or five hard ones," and offering along with it his free recipe, "how to pluck a chicken without losing the *pupik*." "Repeat after me," he said, standing in the spotlight at the Majestic in his black professor's cape and waxed mustache, eyes glittering, "*Gey avec, gey avec, gey vayt avec.*" Hard times notwithstanding, the house was full. People liked to laugh. And my father's problem was now not so much getting the stars to appear, though it still meant urging each one personally, and waiting around backstage at the Latin Quarter or the Copacabana, as finding a place for the lesser-known actors to show off their talents. That year, a young man wearing a beret and carrying a violin wandered around backstage saying, "Take my wife—please," a line that my father didn't find so amusing.

And no sooner had my father taken his bow, spiffy as always in his tuxedo—"Don't you think he looks like Ronald Colman?" Julia whispered. "Clark Gable," I said sternly—this time with his shoulder encircled by the arm of Walter Huston, who was appearing in *Knickerbocker Holiday*, than he began worrying about his Purim play. After which there would be Passover, with its five yizkors and a rousing sermon for each, and the need to discuss finer points of Talmudic interpretation with his colleagues at the Knesset Harabonim and Rabbi Lekhem in Georgia. "You're calling Rabbi Lekhem in *Georgia*?" my mother said. "Clara, in the Midrash rabbis talk to each other across three centuries." And meanwhile Anna Goldman got married, and Seymour Katz was finally bar mitzvahed, only to be supplanted by his brother, Lenny, this one an aficionado of pistachio nuts, and Tippy Klein's young married sister died of pneumonia at the age of twenty-two. Which wasn't to mention a growing round of banquets and testimonial dinners, which my mother refused to attend with him, saying her hair wasn't right or her dress was wrong, though he had been honored by being asked to give the invocation or benediction: "O Lord, Who dwellest on high, bless this assemblage of the members, officers and friends of the Motion Picture Pioneers with the fruit of Your goodness." "We thank Thee, O Lord, for giving us this great humanitarian, Harry Brandt. It is for his years of outstanding service on Broadway and to mankind in general that we honor him tonight." "Bless the Sports Lodge of B'nai B'rith . . . the Young Man's Philanthropic League . . . the Negro Actors Guild. . . ." "Eternal God, we thank Thee for the spirit of friendship and close harmony which prevails at this dinner of the West Side Chamber of Commerce. Bless our distinguished guests of honor, Mr. John D. Rockefeller III, and Miss Helen Hayes. . . ."

When he had typed this last one out at home, on stationery from Grossinger's, he had paused, shaken his head, and called Yosel over. Yosel had given it an expert glance, crossed out "close harmony" and put in "mutual purpose." "I liked 'harmony' better," my father said, smiling ruefully, but yielding. Yosel, after all, had not only been a journalism major, but was now working in the publicity department of Paramount Pictures, his job courtesy of Barney Balaban, another member of the shul. What made my father's life a bit more difficult was that Julia, too, had become involved in show business, in a manner of speaking. In addition to going on a diet, to Clara's shock and horror, she had thrown herself into choral reading at Washington Irving High School. "Fat black bucks in a wine-barrel room,/Barrel-house *kings*, with feet unstable,/Sagged and reeled and pounded on the table . . . Boomlay, boomlay, boomlay, BOOM," went Julia all day long, while my father's benedictions and invocations sagged in his typewriter.

Early in April Rabbi Lekhem came up north for an operation. It was to have taken place on a Saturday, but Rabbi Lekhem insisted on putting it off until after the sabbath. My father walked up to Mount Sinai Hospital to visit him. They had met in New York before when Rabbi Lekhem came to see one of his daughters, now married to a rabbi, or to order one of his black Prince Albert coats, and now the tears sprang into my father's eyes as he entered the room and saw the old patriarch in his hospital gown, long beard extended onto the tight white sheet.

Rabbi Lekhem frowned. "You walked so far on shabbos, Beril?"

"I rested for ten minutes at Radio City," my father said. "Also, one must remember that Manhattan is an island and has no city gates."

"Oy, Beril," Rabbi Lekhem said, weakly shaking his head and laughing. "That's quite an answer."

My father beamed, like a yeshiva boy who has just received the highest approbation. He told the rabbi that they were saying a *mishebeyrach* at the Actors Temple every day, a prayer for his swift recovery, Eddy Duchin, Benny Baker, and Harry Richman included, and then they settled down and talked about Slobodka.

A week before Passover my father took my mother and Julia and me down to the Lower East Side to do our shopping for the holiday. In fact, it was his forty-fifth birthday, but we were not allowed to mention it. Julia and I had borrowed money from Sookie to buy him a black and white striped rep tie, like President Roosevelt's, and he had accepted it with a curt nod, frowning, not because he minded being associated with President Roosevelt, which he took quite lightly, but because his birthday was the one day he could be counted on to be irritable and depressed. On his fortieth birthday, Yossie had given him a copy of *Life Begins at Forty*, and this he had put alongside his jokebooks. With my mother there was no problem because she didn't know when her birthday was.

As we emerged from the subway, the streets were crowded with pushcarts and Jews hawking their wares. For weeks now my mother had been making agitated preparations for the holiday, climbing up on a step stool to consider her Passover dishes, which my father had got from the same manufacturer who provided the "Screeno" display in the lobby of the Tivoli, counting her silver, saying, "*Noch yom tov, noch yom tov*—after Pesach," to every suggestion put to her, including that we go to the circus. The fact that my father had invited Barney Ross, the welterweight champion, to the first seder, had absolutely knocked her for a loop. "A prizefighter we need yet?" "He was in shul saying kaddish for his mother. Believe me, Clara, behind those fists, he's a good Jewish boy." "*Fists?*"

Now she was itching to get started on the food shopping. But my father proceeded calmly into a bookstore on Henry Street, a tiny dark nook with large flaking leather tomes lying slantwise along the shelves, like the ones in Yossie's sleeping alcove. While my mother stood by in an agony of impatience, and my father spoke with the proprietor in Hebrew, Julia and I peered into the dark, dirty glass cases at menorahs, mezuzas, goblets, Torah ornaments, candlesticks, and at the little artifacts from Palestine that my father bought as prizes for the Talmud Torah—miniature Torah scrolls in satin cases, pendants of the Star of David, olive-wood penholders set with little beads through which a person squinting with one eye could see the Wailing Wall in Jerusalem. My father ordered some books, and then in honor of his birthday, though he didn't say so, bought us all presents. For me a little bronze replica of the Ten Commandments to wear on a chain, and also an olive-wood penholder, though I never won any prizes in Hebrew School, which I hated almost as much as P.S. 17; for Julia a silver filigreed mezuza; and for my mother a painting on black velvet of another mother reading a letter from her children. The picture immediately brought tears to my mother's eyes. Before she could start to cry about it in earnest, my father quickly hustled us out onto the street where he got us hot sweet potatoes from a cart owned by a tattered vendor who wore gloves with the top half of the fingers missing. Then we went to a pickle stall, a fish stall, Gertel's Bakery for *mandelbrot* and macaroons, Saperstein's for nuts and dried fruits, then a butcher shop. As Julia and I quarreled about whose presents were better—"Fight about it after *yom tov*," my mother advised us nervously— my father expertly discussed cuts of meat, and then we made a detour through several jam-packed streets to a dilapidated building which a Yiddish sign said was the Yankov Yosef Yeshiva. My father darted up the old stone steps and rang the bell. An old man with a stained and frayed vest answered. They exchanged "*Sholem aleichem*"s. The old man invited him in, but my father shook his head. "Just say Beril was here," he said, pressing a rolled-up wad of bills into the man's hand. He repeated this performance at several more poor and run-down yeshivas, looking more and more depressed and shaking off my questions, and then cheered up at what he had saved for last because it was the best treat of all. The candy store, where we bought pounds of hard candies from Europe, a "kosher salami" made of marzipan, and boxes of brightly colored fruit jellies. "What color is this one, Daddy?" I said, teasing him. "Brown?" "It's red! And this one?" pointing to a green. "I don't know. Gray?" "My father is color-blind," I said proudly to the proprietor, really wanting to say that it was his birthday and that my father always bought us presents on his birthday. "Color-blind?" "A wonderful thing, a real *gedileh*," my mother said. "So where do you come from, lady?" the proprietor asked her. "New York," she said loftily, as if the Lower East Side and anything that wasn't Forty-seventh Street was Brooklyn.

The previous night I had helped my father look for un-leavened bread, *chometz*, equipped with a candle and a feather, searching out every last little cache of crumbs that my mother had rolled up in scraps of newspaper and hidden in various dark corners of the apartment. We had set fire to them, and dropped them flaming into the sink. The next morning, since everything was now kosher for Pesach, and my mother was terrified that I would touch the wrong dish, I had taken two buttered matzos and two hard-boiled eggs along with me for lunch, which I ate at the study table in the *beth hamedresh*, listening to the singsong of two old men poking their thumbs over the Talmud. This first day as always, the matzos tasted deli-cious. By the end of the eight days, as I knew from expe-rience, my stomach would crackle, and I would have given my soul for one portion of Harvard beets at the Au-tomat, or one piece of that now literally forbidden fruit, a jelly apple from the penny arcade on Broadway. The cir-cus at Madison Square Garden, which we had all finally gone to, was only a faded dream, with its pink cotton candy and the dazzling trapeze artists and red-nosed clowns, and the freak show we had visited downstairs beforehand, familiarly greeting some of Mildred's dental patients.

But now at home, there was the hush and smell of the holiday in the air. The dining-room table, cleared for once of Hebrew typewriter, sundry books and papers, broken crayons, and bridal paper dolls, had been covered with a white damask cloth, and set with the *pesachdike* "Screeno" dishes, candles, Haggadahs, seder plate, and an embroidered blue satin matzo cover. In his long white robe and square white yarmulke, leaning back against the bed pillows on his chair, my father, now a king, looked at his guest, Barney Ross, who was attired in what appeared to be a navy blue bar mitzvah suit, as was Yosel, and at my mother, who had hastily and reluctantly removed the apron from her light blue crepe *yom tov* dress, decorated with bugle beads across the chest, in which she celebrated everything from Shemini Atzereth to Tisha B'av. He thought of the rebbetzins in the old country, of their laces and pearls and silks and proud bearing, and wished that she would go with Anita to buy a few dresses in a department store. But she grudged herself finery, grudged him the opportunity to buy her any, even on credit, insisting that the children came first—by which she did not always mean Mildred and Sarah. The girls looked nice enough, however, in their silk print shirtwaist dresses, left over from their twin days. Julia too, who was wearing black, not exactly the symbol of joy, but she thought it made her look thinner. I was scratching at my new organdy Shirley Temple dress from Plotkin's.

But it was time for the seder to begin. Truly a king, he

lifted his silver goblet and we all stood up to say kiddush over the wine, I proudly holding a miniature replica of his large cup. We sat down again, drinking the Palestinian Malaga, of which he was very proud. Then, ceremonially rinsing his hands, he passed a bit of parsley about for us all to dip in salt water and eat. The rest of the traditional items on the seder plate, which he now lifted symbolically and then put down again, would wait until we had finished reading the first half of the Haggadah. The *maror*, in memory of the bitterness of the slavery in Egypt, actually fresh horseradish which Yosel had grated in the kitchen, a man's job, through which he had wept bitter tears; the *haroset*, resembling mortar, which my father himself always made, chopping apples and nuts and adding wine to make a paste; the roasted chicken neck in memory of the ancient sacrifices in the Temple; the baked egg, a symbol of mourning for its destruction. He slid the center matzo from the blue embroidered cover, wrapping it in a napkin and making it into the *afikomen*, which he hid under his pillow where I would be sure to find it later. Clara could hardly sit still. She kept glancing back toward the kitchen, and then apprehensively at Barney Ross's fists, which were resting innocently enough on the table. I was looking more and more itchy in my organdy. He uncovered the matzo. "This is the bread of affliction which our ancestors ate in Egypt," and with a hard look at Clara, "let *all* who are hungry come and eat. . . ." Then he nodded his head to me, the signal I had been waiting for. I stood up and began to recite the Four Questions, one of the high points of my year, translating from Yiddish into Hebrew in a singsong voice, as he had taught me. "*Tateh, ich vil dir fregn fir kashes. Di ershte kashe iz . . .*"

"That's some head she has on her shoulders," Barney Ross said when I had finished.

My father, taking this as a personal compliment, gave a short pleased nod, creased the page of his large Haggadah, indicating that we were to follow along in our small ones, and began.

"*Avodim hayinu l'pharo b'mitzraim* . . . As our ancestors were slaves to Pharaoh in Egypt . . ."

Clara nodded approvingly. The word *slave* appealed to her.

Afterward we all sat back in a stupor. The chopped liver, the matzo ball soup, the roast chicken and matzo meal kugel, the tsimmes, the compote had come from my mother. The fruit piled up in the cut crystal bowl was a gift from Barney Ross. "What else can you bring a rabbi that you know it's safe for him to eat?" he had said, entering with two huge brown paper bags. A point well taken, though it might have been made of wax for all our present intention of eating it. The table was littered with matzo crumbs. We had all drunk our four cups of wine, recited the story of the Four Sons, considered the words of Rabbi Eliezar, Rabbi Akiba, and Rabbi Gamaliel, enumerated the plagues, sung "Dayenu" so loudly and in such disharmony that Barney Ross winced as if he had caught a right to the chin, opened the door for Elijah the Prophet, who as usual failed to make himself visible, excoriated the Egyptians, recited the Great Hallel, wished ourselves in Jerusalem, finished up with "Chad Gadya," and now emerged into the fifth round with Tony Canzoneri.

"So when he left himself wide open like that, I knew I

had him. I led with a right, then a left, then a short up-
percut. . . ."

My father, chin in hand, making a little pile of matzo
crumbs, listened intently. " 'A mighty hand and an out-
stretched arm,' " he said thoughtfully, "the story of Jewish
history." Almost too drunk to keep my eyes open, I
leaned my head on Sookie's shoulder, thinking about the
Charlie McCarthy doll my father had promised me in return for the stolen *afikomen* and how I would be a great
ventriloquist. Barney Ross, except for his broken nose,
was quite handsome, and even describing the knockout
punch, so soft-spoken that my mother had stopped looking worried, recoiling only when he shadow-boxed. Fight
over, my father offered some Palestinian slivovitz all
around. It was a hundred proof and Barney Ross fell into
a coughing fit. "It's also good for cuts and bruises," my
father said helpfully.

"Well," the fighter said when he had recovered, "this is
quite a family you have here. Are these girls twins?"

"Not exactly," my father said.

"Twins run in my father's family, though," I explained.

"And you must be in high school?" he said to Julia.

"Washington Irving. I intend to go to Hunter College,
like my sisters before me."

"And what do you do?" he asked Yossie.

"I'm in publicity at Paramount Pictures."

"That's a pretty important job."

"He even knows the man who cranks the camera for the
Fox Movietone News," I said.

"I don't plan to stay at Paramount forever, though,"
Yossie said, smiling at me indulgently.

"No?"

"I'm going to take time out to write a novel."

My father's eyes widened, as if he had just heard of an extra plague. In the midst of a depression, Yosel was planning to quit his job and write a *novel?* With a puzzled look, Barney Ross turned to my father for guidance. "It's like the fight game, Barney," my father said quickly, trying to eke out a smile. "When it gets to you, it gets to you."

No sooner were the Passover dishes put away than my mother again became preoccupied with the *cochaleyn.* Also I, who wrote a poem beginning, "Good-bye all, I'll be back in the fall." Julia was not coming with us this year. She regarded it as too childish, and was going to work as a cashier at the Strand Theater, where she expected to meet ushers. Mildred and Sarah were once more trying their luck at an adult camp. The summer passed quietly. Occasional weekends, leaving the shammos in charge, my father visited me and my mother. Napping in the hammock, he closed his good ear to the sounds of the women quarreling in the kitchen, or of my mother urging me to eat. "People are starving in Europe!" "It's not *my* fault." "Look at Julia." "I don't ever want to look at Julia." He also went to a few baseball games with Sam Rosh, Cathrael's nephew, rooting passionately for his Yankees whether he was at Yankee Stadium or the Polo Grounds, and took Sam to see *You Can't Take It with You,* which he enjoyed, though the peculiar family struck a bit too close to home. By Labor Day everybody was back again, Mildred and Sarah having failed once more to find any potential husbands, and Julia without having met any ushers. Whether or not Yosel had a serious girl friend was a mystery to everyone since, aside from an occasional unsettling allusion to his novel, the boy kept his business to himself. Clara wasn't in a hurry for Yosel to get married anyway, only the girls. The High Holidays came and went, and then it was time for my father's contract to be renewed. He waited out the meeting in his office, sick to his stomach. When it was over, he had won again. Ely Kapetsky had done his best to make trouble, and had failed. But he hated this whole humiliating business of contracts. What was he—a spiritual leader, or a day laborer? Once more my father thought about enlisting in the Army as a chaplain, or starting all over again in Palestine. And then he remembered his large brood at home, and his actors, always his actors.

"Rabbi—?" Ernie, the new Negro janitor at the shul, said, taking messages one afternoon. "Some show people out on Long Island called. They want you to perform a wedding next Sunday."

"Where's Anita?"

"She's helping Mrs. Birstein buy a corset."

My father nodded, sighing, and changed the subject. "So tell me, Ernie—sit down for a minute—how do you like working here?"

Ernie smiled. "Well, nobody wants to be a janitor."

"No, of course not."

"But it's nice meeting all the actors. And then I get all those holidays off. I mean, if it's not Labor Day, it's Rosh Hashanah."

"That was a beautiful succa you made. Beautifully decorated."

"You liked the Indian corn?"

"A very nice touch, even if it didn't go with Mrs. Goldman's gefilte fish. How was your gig last night?"

"Great. Thanks for the afternoon off. I had to go all the way out to a club in New Jersey."

"Don't mention it. . . . The trumpet is a biblical instrument, you know."

" 'Joshua fit de battle ob Jericho.' "

"I also like 'Go Down Moses,' " my father said, nodding. "Listen, Ernie, would you like a schnapps before services?"

"Okay."

Ernie took a bottle of Scotch, a gift of Leon and Eddie's, from the stationery closet, and poured out two shots in paper cups.

"*L'chaim*," my father said, holding on to his yarmulke as he threw his head back.

"*L'chaim*," Ernie said, holding on to his yarmulke also.

"Well, I'd better make that call."

"And I'd better get that *beth hamedresh* ready for *mincha*."

Telling Ernie he would be down in a minute, my father dialed the number Ernie had left for him.

"We understand you're a show business rabbi," the man at the other end of the wire said.

"In a manner of speaking. What can I do for you?"

"Are you free the twenty-eighth?"

"The date is all right," my father said, "but are you both Jewish?"

"They're both Jewish. Don't worry about it."

"They? To whom am I speaking then?"

"My name is Skip Fefferman," the man said hastily, "but you don't know me."

"Why aren't they calling me themselves?"

"They're shy."

"Shy about getting married?"

"Shy about calling you. They're show people, Rabbi, and you know how most synagogues feel about show people."

"Yes," my father said. "Yes, I do know," and took down the time and directions. It would mean a long trip out on the train carrying his heavy portable *chupa* and rabbinical robe, but that wasn't the problem. Ernie, after all, went out to New Jersey carrying his trumpet. No, there was something about that man's voice that made him uneasy. He tried to persuade himself that it was all in a good cause. Then he went downstairs to tell Ernie that, though his job as a janitor would remain the same, maybe he would like being called super, the super of the whole place.

There was just time to give Lenny Katz a quick bar mitzvah lesson that Sunday morning before he took the train to Long Island. Aside from an addiction to pistachio nuts, which reddened his bitten fingertips, Lenny was as unlike his terrible brother, Seymour, as two brothers could be. A sweet boy, with straight black hair, a pimpled forehead, and earnest brown eyes. Eyes which I looked into soulfully as he stood at the door saying good-bye to my father when the lesson was over and, by necessity, to me.

"So, you see, Lenny," my father said, glancing over at me from time to time, "it's not enough to learn how to read your portion of the Bible, you must read this *maftir* with understanding. You're fortunate in that yours is about Jacob and his dream. And such a dream. A ladder all the way up to heaven, with the angels of God ascending and descending. And God saying, 'I am with thee, and will keep thee wherever thou goest.' Which is why Hosea says, 'O Israel, return to the Lord, thy God.' Meaning, remember God's promise that He will always watch over us. A wonderful thought to hold on to, isn't it?"

Lenny nodded seriously, nibbling at a reddish fingernail.

"Well, anyway," my father said, "I'll try to get over to the penny arcade and make that record for you next week. It's too bad your voice is cracking now, but that's the way life is sometimes."

"—au revoir, Lenny. Or should I say adieu?"

"What? Oh, so long, Hon."

My father turned to look over his shoulder as I quickly sat down at the dining-room table and started scribbling away in my funeral chapel diary, sighing, biting my pencil, gazing dreamily at the spot where Lenny had stood. Wasn't I too young to have crushes on boys? Still, if I was going to sit around pouring my heart out, maybe he should buy me a better diary to do it in. A red leather one, he thought for some reason, with a gilt clasp.

On the train to Long Island, he sat meditating on Lenny's Haftorah, even if I was meditating on Lenny. "I will not leave thee until I have done that which I spoke to thee of." Which meant, though he hadn't yet gone into it with Lenny, but as the sages said, that the earth was full of the glory of God, and that every spot of earth could be a gate of heaven. And then, he thought, descending at Great Neck, of the shy show business couple whom he was about to unite in matrimony. Shy? As he entered the large crowded hall, he was suddenly assaulted by bright lights, clamoring reporters, whirring newsreel cameras. "Right this way, Rabbi," a man with sleek black hair parted in the middle, unmistakably Skip Fefferman, advised him. My father looked to the far end of the room where the bridal pair awaited him. His heart sank. Then he squared his shoulders, picked up the suitcase with his robe and portable *chupa*, and went forward.

"He was a *Jewish* midget!" my father cried. "Who else was supposed to marry them?"

"I don't know," Mr. Kapetsky said. "Maybe some other faker."

"Faker?"

"We have to see your face in the newsreels yet? It's not bad enough that the morning service is late so your *actyoren* can sleep?"

"It's an extra morning service."

"That in your Journal, the Gulden people tell us to put their mustard on our ham? That there's another ad that says 'To the Rabbi with love from Toots'?"

"Toots Shor. That's the way he signs his name."

"Such a person shouldn't even have a name. Come, Ely."

"I just wanted to leave you this," Ely said, smirking. "It's a letter I wrote to your great rabbi, Wolf Margolies of the Knesset Harabonim."

My father waited a moment until after they had left and picked up the carbon.

"To the Assembly of Hebrew Orthodox Rabbis, Gentlemen: . . . I was married December 30, 1928. At that time there was considerable discontent rampant due to the pernicious activities of this supposedly Rabbi. Since that time his conduct has led to more discontent and a disgraceful condition among the Jews in our neighborhood. I consider this one of the worst individuals . . ."

"Daddy, Daddy!" I cried when he came home. "You're playing in the newsreel at the Tivoli!"

"*Shah,* Chana," my mother said, looking at his face. "*Shah.*"

"But, Beril, what for?" old Rabbi Margolies said, having handed him a carbon copy of yet another letter: ". . . We wish to inform you that it is below the dignity of our Rabbinical Assembly to enter into correspondence of such a nature as you suggest. We have known Bernard Birstein as a full-fledged and ordained rabbi for a good many years. He is our executive secretary. We wish to assure you that your communication did not alter in the least our high esteem for Rabbi Birstein, and that in the future . . ."

"Reb Velvel, I appreciate what you said—"

"There's nothing to appreciate."

"But I still want to do it all over again."

"Beril, you already have a *smicha* from Slobodka."

"It's not the *smicha.* I want to be tested."

"By whom?"

"By you. By Rabbi Trainen. By Rabbi Lekhem by telephone. By everyone."

"You are so stubborn," Reb Velvel said. "So young."

"Test me," my father said.

It was one of the happiest times of his life. He studied and studied, taking down the large flaking tomes from the bookshelves and slapping the covers to get the dust out of

them, so that in the living room motes danced in the sunshine around the snakeplants and dime store ashtrays.
"Every person in every generation," he said to me, "must
regard himself as having been personally freed from
Egypt," though it wasn't Pesach. On the appointed day,
dressed in his cutaway as he had been for his naturalization, he went downtown and there sat before Rabbi Margolies and his group. In his shiny black gabardine,
thoughtfully parting his white beard in the middle with
both hands, Rabbi Margolies asked him the hardest questions he could think of, and so did they all, laughing and
crying at the same time. A few days later *smicha* after
smicha arrived in the mail, written in Hebrew script and
adorned with rabbinical seals, until he had a dozen of
them.

And still it was not enough. There was no more talk by
Ely Kapetsky and his doddering father of forcing him to
resign, though they now stood apart from the rest of the
congregation at services, davening louder and faster than
anyone. But still, all he was left with was the rest of a
two-year contract. And after that another? Then another?
He could not live this way. A rich congregation in Cleveland wrote, asking him to become their rabbi. A permanent position, and a good one. The synagogue was large
and beautiful; he would have a sisterhood, a men's club,
a Hebrew school well-staffed with teachers, assistants ga-
lore. Cleveland was famous for its well-established Jewish
community, the home of the esteemed Rabbi Abba Hillel
Silver. He considered the proposal long and hard, thinking of the good life he would at last be able to offer his

is that of the humanitarian and he plays it to the hilt, bringing comfort and solace to Christian and Jew alike.' "

A very nice mention indeed. And speaking of acts, Sullivan had said privately that he would help line some up for the next benefit. His formula: "Open big, have a good comedy act, put in something for the children, keep the show clean." For this last stipulation, Ed had quickly apologized, but then of course, he had forgotten. . . . Perhaps he should present Ed with a little gift, a gold mezuza for his key chain perhaps, or maybe something more original, something inscribed, that Mrs. Sullivan, a Jew, would appreciate also.

"Oh, and Red sent you a lovely thank-you note. He said it was short, sweet, and painless, and he enclosed a donation for the shul because you wouldn't take any fee."

"He's a good boy," my father said. "Anything else?"

"No, that's it. Oh, yes, where should I put the picture Congressman Kennedy sent us?"

"Maybe in the Talmud Torah." My father sighed. "Do you have your pad? Take a letter. 'To the Honorable Michael J. Kennedy. Dear Congressman Kennedy: Thank you for the beautiful gift of Howard Chandler Christy's representation of "The Signing of the Constitution." It is a gift that will bring inspiration to all who behold it. Young and old, rich and poor—' " No, that didn't sound right. He would have Yosel look it over before he sent it. "I'll finish it tomorrow. . . . How did you and Irving like *Three Men on a Horse* last night?"

"It was wonderful, Rabbi, thank you."

"Did you go backstage like I told you?"

"Yes, we did. He knew you."

"A very fine actor, Sam Levene," my father said, wishing to absent himself a little longer from that nest of Bol-

wife and four daughters, the good steady job he could find Yosel, who would maybe forget about writing novels. (And Clara, what would they make of Clara? This he did not permit himself to dwell on.) But also thinking of himself. Wasn't a man of forty-six entitled to a measure of security in this terrible strife-torn world? A world in which Hitler had already invaded Austria, and Chamberlain, Daladier and Mussolini were ready to give up Czechoslovakia? He prayed for peace, though he did not believe it was possible, and also for personal guidance, though he knew it would have to come from within himself. Day after hot day he walked his beat, to Broadway and beyond, past the Gaiety Delicatessen—"How's your mother's gall bladder, Ted? Still bothering her?"—and the Loew's State Theater—"Lou, tell your daughter she's got a nice boy there"—and the stage door of the Palace, through which had come so much talent, trying not to see it as Broadway, but as a bad place to bring up a family.

He told the congregation in Cleveland he was thinking it over, thinking harder when Sarah and Mildred came back from their two-week vacation even more exhausted than they were from their jobs. Mildred, having completed her two years at Hunter in the day, now also worked full time and went to school at night, no longer able to major in art. He could not bear to see the girls so tired all the time, flinging themselves across the bed for a few minutes' nap when they came home for lunch, Mildred in her nurse's uniform and white shoes and stockings. Somehow he would have to see to it that Julia, whose turn it was next, would stay in college full time.

"I'm not going back to that *cochaleyn* anymore," Clara announced on her return, unwrapping the newspapers from all her pots and pans. "Why should I cook and clean all summer when I cook and clean all winter? I was a slave to my father, and now—"

"Next year, you'll go to a hotel," my father said. "God willing."

"How? With what?"

"We'll find a way," my father said. "Channele, you like the country now, don't you?"

"I don't know. It's very lonesome there."

"You're still not used to fresh air."

"Yes, but Daddy, then this apartment looked so *small* when I got back."

My father looked around. It was small. Three girls in one tiny bedroom, another on the dining-room couch, his only son, his pride and joy, in a dark alcove. He was decided.

Kol Nidre night, he stood on the bima in his long white robe and square white yarmulke, and silver embroidered tallis, feeling good-bye if not saying good-bye. The congregation was still filing in. From upstairs he heard the uncertain flush of the toilet outside the Ladies Balcony, from next door at the rehearsal hall, a herd of tap dancers clomping away in unsteady rhythm, being yelled at or made to repeat. Good-bye rotten plumbing, good-bye scrounging around for minyans, good-bye Miss Bohan and Tammany Hall, and kids running in to desecrate. Upstairs, Belle Baker came in and took her seat, causing all heads to turn. Then Sophie Tucker entered, creating even more of a stir. The two of them seemed to be vying over whose hat was more outlandish. Belle Baker took out her handkerchief, preparing to cry in advance. Sophie Tucker whipped out an even larger, lacier one.

He signaled the congregation to rise, and nodded to the cantor, whom he had hired especially for the holidays, and to the president, and together they opened the ark, taking out three Torahs. "With the consent of God," my father proclaimed in Hebrew, "and with the consent of the congregation, and with the consent of the heavenly tribunal, and with the consent of the tribunal here on earth, we herewith declare that it is permitted to pray together with those who have transgressed." My father, holding the smallest Torah, for they were heavy, then descended and led the procession up and down the aisle, singing as he always did, seven times, *"Or zorua latsadik v'lishrey leyv simcha.* Light is sown for the righteous and gladness for the upright in heart." The men leaned over to touch the Torahs with the tips of their talesim and kiss them, and there were tears upstairs and down. When he had finished the last repetition of the verse in a hoarse crescendo, his voice finally breaking, there were tears in his own eyes too. Stepping forward, the cantor began the Kol Nidre prayer. "All vows, bonds, devotions, promises with which we have vowed, sworn, devoted and bound ourselves . . ."

The cantor had a beautiful tenor voice, full of feeling, and my father was glad he had engaged him. Such a strange haunting prayer too, all in Aramaic, except for one Hebrew phrase, and pondered over for centuries. And what did it mean? That our vows had no validity? No, but that some of them through God's intervention, as with Abraham and Isaac, it would be impossible for us to fulfill. When the chazan had finished, he slapped his prayer book for order, and spread his notes on the lectern.

Sarah, in the flush of her young womanhood, clearly felt flushes for Harry. And why should Fanny have two sweethearts and she none? She rearranged her flowered chiffon skirts, laughed, sang love songs on the long summer nights, and soon Harry Pollack was sitting on the swing between her and Fanny. "I don't like it, Beril," Clara said to him one evening in the kitchen, making a herring into a spiral and jamming it into a jar of yellow water. "It's not right." "What's not right?" "Fanny's older. She should get married first." "Believe me, Clara," Beril said, smiling, "Sarah's not getting married yet. She's just having a good time." At the words "good time," Clara sank into an even deeper depression, blowing her nose in one of Beril's handkerchiefs and stuffing it into her apron pocket. When they walked out onto the porch, she sat down on the top step and fanned herself between her legs. "*Sheyn vi di levoneh,*" Sarah sang. "Lovely as the moon." Where the others relaxed, Clara shvitzed.

As a respite from the heat, Beril took his entourage to Coney Island. Clara made sandwiches and packed them into shoe boxes but refused to come along. At the beach Beril paid for the lockers, and with keys dangling from their wrists, they found a place to spread their blanket. The young aunts ran cavorting toward the ocean's edge, and coming back from the water couldn't find the blanket. Beril waved to them, sitting with the children in his bathing suit, the top white, like an undershirt, the trunks black with a red, white, and black striped belt in between. Alex and Hymie ogled girls, the children dug holes. They ate sandy sandwiches, and then returned home on the subway, saving the shoe boxes for next time. At their hilarious entrance, Clara looked at them tight-lipped and proceeded to smear the children with Noxzema,

"Ten days ago, on Rosh Hashanah," he said, looking out at his congregation as if for the last time, "we celebrated the world's birthday. A marvelous event by any standards. But what kind of a world? you might ask. A world where Nazism runs rampant, and Jews are persecuted, and people are starving to death—one third of a nation is ill-housed, ill-clothed, ill-fed—and war clouds hang over Europe. A terrible, terrible mess. Yet, let us consider: Is this the world God created? The world that we read about in Genesis? The world with its heavens and earth and seas, and seeds and herbs and trees and gardens, and every living creature? A world so beautiful that when the Almighty, blessed be He, finished, the angels wept to see His handiwork? No, my friends, that world was God's world. And in doing our best to destroy it, we have substituted this one. 'Don't corrupt and desolate My world,' God said to Adam, 'for if you corrupt it, there is no one to set it right after you.' And we went ahead and did it, anyhow."

He looked out at his congregation, all of them crestfallen. Particularly Hank Danning, and Barney Ross, and young Milton Berle, whose mother was in the balcony. Tonight, they were chastened and quiet. By tomorrow, they would be thinking about the World Series, and the daily double at Jamaica.

"But if it is in man's power to destroy," he said, smiling more kindly, "it is also in his power to create. Not as God creates. Man is not God, though he was made in His image. And not alone. No, *we* here on earth can create only by joining together. As Jews we are never alone. God does not like the person who walks alone. We need a minyan to pray. Our entire Jewish religion is based on a sense of community. All our prayers are in the plural form. But in saying them, we must also bring to them a sense of commitment.

"It is said that in Athens, the ones who were punished after a war were those who did not take part on one side or the other. To put it another way, and as Hank Danning will tell you, you can't get to first base without going to bat. But go to bat for what?

"There are many thoughts of death connected with these High Holidays, and with synagogues in general. We come on the anniversary of a parent's death to say kaddish, tomorrow we will say yizkor. And this is right. Not until our thoughts themselves are put to sleep, do we or should we give up our beloved dead. There in our hearts we cling to them, though it break our hearts to do so. But there is more to our religion than that. There is joy as well as grief. In our prayers we say thanks for everything: the new moon, the sun, the stars, a piece of bread, a cup of wine. For with this wonderful world, *His* wonderful world, God gave us the capacity to enjoy it. He gave us the greatest gift of all. Life itself."

He pushed away his notes.

"Dear friends, don't be miserly with this gift, I beg you. Spend life recklessly on the great and good things. On truth, on beauty, on goodness. Give it away for friendship and love. Fling it away on your devotion to the ideals of our people. *Forget the point of no return!*"

He ended soon after with a plea for funds. "We don't say blessed are the poor," he advised them wryly, as the pledges started rolling in, and the rest of the congregation gasped at the famous names, as they always did. Jack Benny, Joe E. Lewis, Tony Martin, Sophie Tucker. Finally, he took his papers from the lectern and sat down. What had he done? "Forget the point of no return"?

Where was "good-bye"? He looked down at his notes, realizing too late that he had said what he meant, but not what he had meant to say. It was good-bye all right, but not to his congregation—to Cleveland.

"Wonderful sermon, Rabbi."
  "Thank you, Red," my father said glumly.
  "Inspirational," Jack Benny told him.
  "Thank you."
  "Spend your life recklessly! *Oy, rebele!*" Sophie Tucker cried, flinging her arms around him, so that he could barely look out over her shoulder.
  "Thank you," my father said.
  Mr. Alter seemed a bit dubious, Mrs. Alter rather more enthusiastic. It did not terribly much matter, since Mr. Alter, aging, was to retire after long years as president. At the next Board of Officers meeting, Mildred's circus dentist and the fight doctor were elected president and vice-president respectively.
  "Listen, Rabbi, don't worry about your next contract," they both said.
  "Thank you," my father sighed, chin in hand, reading the newspaper, Cleveland almost forgotten, though the occasional thought of it still stabbed him to the heart. Obviously, a certain kind of good life would never be his. In any case, how could he worry about his own fate when the world news grew worse each day? Hitler was on the march, and not all the Chamberlains in the world would be able to stop him. His family in Russia had not been heard from in some time. He prayed for peace and knew there would be war. In April Hitler broke the Munich Pact, and in May President Roosevelt opened the New

York World's Fair. He took me out there on the Flushing subway line, and smiled at me with a sweet sadness when I explained to him that the Trylon and the Perisphere were symbols of peace. At the Heinz exhibit I got a little green pickle to pin on my lapel, pickles were kosher, and then we went to the Aquacade produced by his friend, Billy Rose, who had given him free tickets. For my sake he pretended to enjoy himself, but I could tell it was only half-hearted. Only Steinmetz Hall truly interested him, with its manmade thunder and lightning. "B'reyshis," he said musingly. " 'In the beginning . . .' "

The next time I went Sookie and Mildred took me, then Julia and Ruthie Katz, Lenny Katz's older sister. "Come on, brat," Julia said, as I stood transfixed outside the Futurama. I was pondering on what Ruthie had just said in passing, that her brother had six toes. On one foot? Each foot? How would this affect my feeling for him? ("I don't know about Lenny Katz," I wrote in my Riverside Memorial Chapel diary. "I don't know whether I love him or hate him.") When Yossie took me, we watched Chaim Gross sculpt a figure out of a piece of wood. In addition to planning his novel, Yossie, who was very artistic, was also interested in sculpting and painting. When I went with my friend Tippy, the kosher-butcher's daughter, we stayed out so late promenading up and down along the Lagoon of Nations, that Tippy's mother almost called the police. ("I wonder about Tippy," I wrote in my diary.) My mother and I spent July at the Hotel Anderson in Monticello, where I starred in a kiddie show, singing, "So you met someone and now you know how it feels. Goody-goody." In August, Germany and Russia signed a non-aggression pact. "Keep that man *away* from *here!*" my father shouted at my mother when Uncle Max called up to explain why. At the beginning of September, the Nazis invaded Poland. That same week, Sarah and Mildred came home from Camp Tamiment.

"I don't believe you," I said to Julia. "Sookie would have told me before anybody."

"Snap out of it," Julia said. "He's coming over, isn't he?"

"They all come over."

"Not like this," Julia said, indicating the dining-room table, which once more had been swept clear of its usual mess, and covered with an embroidered cloth, all in multicolored cross-stitches, one corner of which I had done myself before getting bored. There were glasses for tea, and preserves, and strudel which my mother had spent days baking, and sponge cake and honey cake and fruit and Scotch from "21" and Canadian Club. The dishes were flowered china, and the fruit knives were pearl-handled. Four chairs had been set in place. "Four chairs match, four people sit," my mother had said firmly—was she actually going to sit down at the table though it wasn't Friday night or Passover?—and the rest of us were more or less to drape ourselves around the scene of the action. My mother, in her bugle-beaded blue *yom tov* dress, bustled in and out hysterically, now to adjust a pearl-handled fruit knife or a plate of strudel, now to remove the sweaters hanging from the handle of the Victrola and stuff them behind the cushions on Mildred's daybed.

"How did she meet this character?" I asked Julia.

"Well, she was on her way to play golf—"

"Sookie plays *golf*?"

"—in her red satin two-piece, and there was this guy sitting under a tree with a book, and he looked up and said, 'C'mere, kid, I want to read you some poetry,' or something cute like that, and she—"

"He's a poet?"

"He's a doctor. What do you think all this fuss is about?"

"A *doctor*? But Mama wants her to marry a doctor."

"*Shah, shah,*" my mother said to no one in particular, pushing Julia and me aside. At the appointed hour the rest of the family filed in, like actors onto a stage set, my father taking the chair with the arms at the head of the table, then Sookie in a red watered silk princess dress with tiny buttons down the front, the chair opposite her ominously empty, then my mother. Millie and Yossie and I retreated to the daybed, and Julia leaned casually against the china closet. My mother sat down, then jumped up again when the bell rang. "No, I'll get it!" I said. "Don't you dare!" Sookie cried, running off to the door.

A few minutes later she ushered in her prize, leading him less like a groom than a lamb to a sacrificial altar. "Come in, come in, Doctor," my father said, rising. "My daughter has told us so much about you." We all rose with him as we did in shul.

"Sandy Pearlman, everybody," Sookie said brightly.

He looked around at us all, stared back for a moment, then handed his hat to Sookie, who passed it lightly to me. I tossed it on the daybed behind me, and stood there with my mouth open, flabbergasted, unable to believe the evidence of my eyes. After all of it, the handsome Walter with the gardenia plant, the dashing Ace with his white silk aviator's scarf, was my beloved sister actually going to marry this, this *doctor*? He was short, stocky, pale-haired, and cold. This man gave enemas.

"Take a seat," my father said cordially, and we all sat down again, except for Julia who remained languidly draped against the china closet.

"I only have a few minutes away from the hospital," Sandy explained.

"I appreciate that fact, Doctor, but I'm glad of this opportunity to meet you."

"Eat something," my mother said.

"I'll just have some tea, thank you."

She bustled in and out of the kitchen with his glass.

"My daughter's told me about your brilliant work," my father said. "In TB, is it? I myself was once a fund raiser for the Jewish Outpatients Sanitarium in Denver. I like the Far West. I enjoy cowboy pictures too."

"Is that so?"

"I hear diathermy can accomplish wonders," Julia remarked.

"Have a piece of strudel," my mother said.

"No, thanks, I—"

"I baked it myself. It's home-baked!"

"Clara, please," my father said with a smile. "And after this residency, I assume you'll be going into private practice?"

"No, not yet. I'm planning to specialize in roentgenology, which means another residency."

"Another residency," my father said, nodding, and tamping down his mustache thoughtfully. "And you feel you can support a wife on—?"

"A hundred dollars a month? No," Sandy laughed. "But Sook's agreed to go on working until I'm finished."

"Sarah's going to go on working after you're married?" my father said, shooting her a sharp glance.

"Only for a little while," Sandy said.

My father looked at Sookie again, who gave him a quick pleading smile.

"Well, I suppose it's the modern way," my father said. "I wish you both the best of everything." He smiled back at Sookie. "You have my blessing."

My mother started to cry.

Sandy looked at his watch. "I'm afraid I—"

"Eat something," my mother said, blowing her nose.

"Don't force him. The doctor clearly doesn't wish to eat," my father said.

"Sook, where did I put my hat?" Sandy asked, looking around.

"His hat! Where's the gentleman's hat?" my father demanded.

With a sick feeling, I reached underneath me. Sandy silently regarded the crushed and battered object, no longer hat, I handed over to him.

"I beg your pardon?" he said, turning.

"I was wondering," my father repeated enthusiastically, "if you enjoy a game of chess."

"I don't believe this," I said to Sookie, after she had closed the door. "I don't believe any of it."

"What don't you believe?" she said dreamily.

"Aren't you the one who liked tall dark men with five o'clock shadow?" I demanded.

"I was."

"Then how could you—?"

"Leave her alone," my father said, leading me off. "Sometimes you have to roll with the punches."

The wedding was set for July 14, the first free Sunday after Shevuoth, and also Bastille Day, which appealed to Sookie's romantic instincts. "Freedom for whom?" Sandy said on one of his subsequent visits, which were brief and infrequent. There was still not much love lost between us. "Why does that kid sit around in her pajamas all day?" he asked one Sunday, looking up from Cathrael's inlaid chess table. "Why doesn't she get some fresh air?" "Check mate! The doctor's right, Channele." "He's not *my* doctor," I said. "When she's not playing Monopoly, she's going to see *Gone With the Wind*," he remarked on another occasion. "Those are all long-term occupations. Doesn't she ever do anything else?" "Sookie, kindly tell your so-called fiancé to mind his own beeswax." "Oh, Honey, *please*—" Julia, of course, liked him. It was typical of her to warm up to such a person. So did Mildred, but I felt that was only because Sandy introduced her to all his doctor friends from the hospital and they and she and Sookie all double-dated together. Yossie seemed to be neutral, but then he was away from home so much it was hard to pin him down on anything. Yossie said any man with four sisters would be away a lot.

It was not, of course, the greatest time in the world to plan on getting married. Britain and France had gone to war, and though Roosevelt had declared our neutrality, it was a strange kind of neutrality. There was even talk that American boys might be drafted, and Yossie, who had wanted to enlist in the Spanish Civil War but had been dissuaded, said he wasn't going to wait for an invitation from a draft board this time. My family spent a great deal of time discussing such matters, and even my mother and father seemed drawn together by the perilous times we were living in.

One day the sound of their quarreling in the kitchen attracted me. I knew they were talking about Sookie because whenever my mother said "she" in that tone of voice, that's who my mother was talking about. It surprised me, because ever since that first awful day when Sandy came to call and I sat on his hat, Sookie had been in very good odor in our house. It was as if all her old sins such as interpretive dancing and wanting to play the violin had been forgiven as youthful foibles. I wondered if she would let me have the gauze tunic and the chamois slippers when she got married. I had a feeling she wasn't going to be using them anymore.

My mother was standing at the stove, rendering chicken fat and frying an onion. I slid in beside my father at the chipped white enamel table. He didn't look very happy to see me.

"Why?" my mother said. "Why does she have to go there?"

"Because it's a custom. The girl's getting married."

"Lily's a custom?"

"She knows where the grave is," my father said.

"Whose grave?" I asked him. "What's this all about?"

"Channele, don't you have any homework?"

"Sarah wants to go to Chicago," my mother said, slicing another onion.

"So why shouldn't she?" I said. "What's wrong with that? It's a major city in the Midwest."

My mother pursed her lips.

"Clara, please," my father said.

My mother spent a few moments gazing distantly at the simmering contents of her frying pan.

"She wants to invite her mother to her wedding," she said finally, turning around. "All right? Now you know?"

"Know what? Invite whose mother to what wedding? What's going on around here, anyhow?"

"Ask Papa."

"Channele, listen," my father said in a pleading voice. "Listen, Channele—"

I listened. And it was awful. Even when it had all been explained to me—and I took weeks getting it straight— "She's not mine," my mother said, "Julia's mine." *Julia?* Julia was my real sister?—I couldn't, I wouldn't believe any of it. How had they dared live those secret lives without me? And how had that shadowy woman whose name I didn't even know died? Nobody told me. Maybe my father had killed her, which was why they kept it so quiet. Maybe he had, in fact, really killed Zayde too. "What are you talking?" my mother said. "Zayde died from old age. Papa made the funeral."

All right. Then maybe murder was a bit far-fetched. Still, many other dark mysteries remained. For example, if my mother wasn't Sookie's real mother, or Mildred's, or Yossie's, then maybe my father wasn't a real rabbi either. The more I thought about it, the more painfully evident this became. He was too young and handsome. He didn't have a beard. He was nice to people and didn't make them do things they didn't want to. Maybe the bad balabatim were right, though I hated them too much to believe that either. And then there was the problem of decorum, seriously lacking in my father's synagogue. Why were the people in our shul always davening away at their own speed, some with voices like cows lowing, talking, laughing, and in the case of the younger women and girls, flirting down from the balcony? This was certainly wrong. I had heard about Temple Emmanuel, I had sneaked into St. Patrick's, and I knew what was what. I decided, finally, that I was the only truly religious person around. "Go to Chicago," I urged Sookie. "Have the courage of your spiritual convictions." She looked at me as if I had gone mad. "She got over that a long time ago, you idiot," Julia explained when Sookie went off to night school. "Daddy told her that she was overinfluenced by *The Dybbuk*, and that her mother was with her in spirit all the time, anyway."

I buried myself in the Psalms, particularly numbers 15 and 121. "Lord, who shall sojourn in Thy tabernacle?/Who shall dwell upon Thy holy mountain?/He that walketh uprightly, and worketh righteousness,/And speaketh truth in his heart," and "I will lift up mine eyes unto the mountains:/From whence shall my help come?", enunciating each word clearly and distinctly as I held forth in the living room, Bible in hand like a teacher in homeroom. But the words did not console me as they had presumably consoled young David, particularly since the thought of homeroom only reminded me of the secular and daily misery of P.S. 17. One day I ate the tapioca pudding I had cooked in Mrs. Sinsheimer's class without first asking my father if tapioca was kosher. Another time, in History, I didn't remember the name of the secretary of the treasury. "Morgenthau," Miss Calahan said clearly, "I don't think your father would be very proud of you at this moment, do you, Anna?" I burst into tears, shaking my head when she demanded I explain what was the matter. My father be proud of me. Let her believe in that impostor, even if I couldn't. It was awful.

In the midst of all this, Cathrael became seriously ill. According to reports his head swelled up. It was diagnosed as a brain tumor. "I knew that woman would kill him in the end," my father said grimly. "It was in the cards." He had a dream that Cathrael would not survive the operation and said as much to Sam Rosh, Easy's cousin, who had introduced him to baseball, when they took the night train to Norfolk together and talked until dawn. "Where's your faith, Uncle Bernard?" Sam said. "Have you no faith that things will come out all right?" "That's not what faith means," my father said, his eyes red from weeping. "I know that my brother will be dead when we get there." He was, and lay in his living room with his head on two bricks.

My father stayed in Norfolk for the seven days of mourning, and more. One bleak afternoon, when we were two women alone in the house, my mother looked at me uneasily and said she wanted to send Fredel a sympathy card, notwithstanding that Fredel had killed Cathrael in the first place. "That's ridiculous. People don't go around giving other people brain tumors." She looked at me with a knowing and bitter smile and we went downstairs to the cigar store, where she picked out a card with embossed flowers all over it, ignoring my recommendation of the one with the stern black border. Not wishing to go through the Landon fiasco all over again, I signed it for her, "Clara Birstein," adding with a certain funereal dignity the words: "Your sister-in-law." . . . "You know what Rosalie Alter said?" I said to Sookie a few mornings later, as we walked down Eighth Avenue past Madison Square Garden and paused across the street from the Automat. "She said her sister Sylvia's marriage brought them even

closer together. And they were very close to begin with."
"That's nice," Sookie said, giving me an absentminded
kiss, and continuing on to the Film Center. I looked at
her slender diminishing back in the red princess coat, and
then turned down Forty-seventh Street, closing my eyes
against the dread, looming sight of P.S. 17. School was
getting even worse, if possible. I hated it. Every day I
wrote in my funeral chapel diary something like, "I hate
school. I hate it. Took a walk with Tippy, who is boy
crazy."

"Anna," Miss Ward said, calling me to her desk that
afternoon and announcing the results of a citywide reading
test to the entire class. "You have the reading ability of a
college freshman. Tell your father." It was the last straw.
I didn't want to tell my father anything. I didn't want my
father's head anymore. I slogged miserably all the way
home, nodding when my mother opened the door and
said, "Papa's home." "Papa's home," she repeated. "I
heard you," I said, bursting into tears. "What's the matter
with you?" "Nothing. It's school. I want to transfer to
where nobody knows me," I said, and went into the living
room where I sat down on the old rose-colored couch, not
even bothering to pat down the long cushion when it bil-
lowed up on either side of me. "I'll get Papa." "Don't you
dare," I said, and waited for him to appear.

He came in unshaven, in slippers, his shirt collarless,
his belt unbuckled. A piece of paper dangled from his
hand.

"What's the matter, *mein kind?* Mama says something's
bothering you."

"It's nothing."

"Nothing?"

{ 185 }

"What are you writing?" I said.

He looked down at the paper. "It's in Hebrew. You won't be able to read it without the dots."

"Show me anyway."

There were a few short lines in Hebrew script. It looked like a poem.

"It's an epitaph," he said. "The first letters will spell his name."

I recognized a *kof*, then a *tof*, then a *reysh*.

"Like a puzzle?"

"Like a puzzle," my father said, "but with all the blank spaces filled in." He laid the piece of paper on Cathrael's inlaid chess table. "So?"

"I told you. Nothing. I just want to transfer out of P.S. 17. I hate that place."

"It's worth it to you for one term? You're graduating in June."

"I don't care."

"All right, I'll speak to Miss Bohan." He looked down at me thoughtfully. "Channele?"

"What?"

"Don't you know that there are more important things than what happens in school?"

"I do know."

"So why are you crying?"

I hesitated. "Because—because Uncle Cathrael died."

He gave me a funny look, and then his eyes filled with tears and he pressed my head against him, where his rumpled shirt met his unbuckled belt.

It was hard to believe that there had ever been such preparations for a wedding. The invitation alone was so crowded there was hardly room for the place and date. "Rabbi and Mrs. Bernard Birstein request the honor of your presence at the marriage of their daughter, Sarah Rachel, to Dr. Alexander William Pearlman, son of Mr. and Mrs. Samuel Maurice Pearlman. . . ." My father engaged the cantor he had so much enjoyed on the High Holidays, who would bring along his own choir, and the Hotel Edison right on Forty-seventh Street donated its Sun Room for the reception, food catered gratis by Trotsky's Kosher Caterers. When the invitations weren't answered soon enough, telegrams flew back and forth, my father's stipulation being that absolutely no Communists or converts were to be among the guests, which took care of Max and Alex and Fanny, though not Big Sarah and Harry and Hymie and Goldie and Hershel and his Goldie and all their children, the children being assigned to the table next to the musicians, all the children except me. "She's never been a child anyway," Sookie said. Actors sent checks. My mother made the point that Alex was saving up to buy the grocery store where he clerked and therefore was on his way to being a capitalist, but my father turned his deaf ear. Easy promised to come up north. Without telling anyone except my mother and father, Sookie sneaked away and had an eye operation. ("Did you really think it made any difference to me?" Sandy said afterward.) When she was all recovered, she went to four different wholesale houses to find the perfect white bridal gown and veil. Bachrach, another connection of my father's, would do the photographs. Mildred and Julia and I went to three other wholesale houses to get our own gowns—"Are you crazy?" I cried. "Me go to Plotkin's at a time like this?"—I finally settling on a long sprigged muslin, whose puffed sleeves I kept pushing off my shoulders in imitation of Scarlett O'Hara. "Scarlett *O'Hara?*" Julia said, falling off the couch laughing. My real sister.

I didn't mind that my graduation was being overshadowed—the less said about P.S. 17 the better, though, no, it really hadn't made sense to transfer out for one term—only that the war news overshadowed everything. Denmark, Norway, Holland, Luxembourg, Belgium all fell. Italy declared war on France and Great Britain. "The hand that held the dagger has *struck* it into the back of its neighbor," we heard Roosevelt say as we all sat raptly around our Philco, which had been moved into the living room. Yossie leaped up and would have enlisted right then and there, if my father had not restrained him. It was a thrilling but worrisome time.

Oddly, when the time came for me to graduate from P.S. 17, I felt an actual pang at leaving the place, and when my father presented the journalism prize to Shirley Ackerman, tears sprang into my eyes. I was valedictorian, and received a valedictorian medal with a blue ribbon to pin on my white graduation dress, plus an illustrated biography of former mayor James J. Walker. Congressman Michael J. Kennedy made the presentation along with a few choice words on the ideals on which our country was founded, and good citizenship in general. I stood beside him on the stage, more or less trying to keep various parts of myself together. I had had my hair set in a pageboy at George's Barber Shop, and it was coming down. So was the hem of the white voile dress that I had sewn in Mrs. Sinsheimer's class and that I had tripped on stepping up to the platform. The fake gardenias at my shoulder were falling off. I was not expected to make a speech in return, but instead, as the color guard dipped their flags, led those in the auditorium in singing the New York City song: "Oh, Watchman of the City gate, how doth our City fare?/Doth any Foeman lurk and wait to pierce Her armour there?" Ending, "Our lives protect New York from harm. Our *deeds* defend Her fame!"—followed by "The Star-Spangled Banner." Afterward, there wasn't much else to do but kiss my father and hang around. Congressman Kennedy stood nearby, gazing off into the distance, flanked by two henchmen, or at least two portly gentlemen in double-breasted suits with their hands in their pockets.

"Hello, Congressman Kennedy," I said. "Thank you for the book and the medal."

"And don't you look pretty in your long white dress and blond curls," he said, beaming at me. And then, before the henchmen had time to nudge him, "—and what's your father doing now? Still in the same business?"

My father closed his eyes. It was a tragic moment. Of all the people an old pol like Michael J. Kennedy could have asked that question, he had had to pick my father's daughter.

"*Du bist meshuga?*" my mother cried to Sookie. "You're going rowing in Central Park today? The morning of your wedding?"

"It's her last crack at freedom," I said, loving Sookie all over again. "But you wouldn't understand such things."

We all four stood facing her in slacks and curlers, even Julia defiant. "Let them go, let them go," my father said, though not approving either—there was a time and a place for everything, and marriage was a serious matter—but understanding our need, for the last time, to be all girls together. It was a hot July morning. We went off to

{ 189 }

the park and spent an hour circling the lake, Sookie rowing, with arms as muscled and tense in her sleeveless blouse as a stevedore's. As usual, a couple of young men in other rowboats flirted with her, and she flirted back, delighted that there were none of the marks of the married woman on her yet. Oh, Sookie, I thought, oh, Sookie, looking at her bright and birdlike, her black cropped hair covered by a red scarf, silhouetted against the dusty green city trees. "Oh, Sookie," I said when we got home, sweaty and sunburned, Sookie's palms so blistered that my mother threw up her own hands. But she had already gone off to shower, and then get dressed in my mother and father's bedroom, which had been made into a kind of bridal bower for the occasion with a sheet spread on the floor to protect her long white veil and train. Easy had just arrived, and I turned my attention to him, as excited to see him as I used to be to see Cathrael. I was worried that there would be some of the mourner about him, some lingering background blackness, but he was smiling and he was still Easy. He had brought me a Japanese backscratcher and offered me five cents an hour to scratch his back for him.

"Well, Uncle," he said as I started, "lose a daughter, gain an extra bed. You can certainly use one."

"We're thinking of moving altogether," my father said. "Polly Adler's lawyer told me about something on Fifty-fourth Street right off Broadway."

"The notorious Polly Adler's lawyer?"

"He comes to shul. I think she used to live in that apartment."

"Then you'll have a lot of extra beds," Easy said.

"Who's Polly Adler?" I asked.

"Scratch."

Sookie emerged and, with my mother trailing after her, went into the living room where her gown and veil could be adjusted and spread to advantage. My father tilted his head thoughtfully.

"What do you think, Papa?" Sookie said.

"It's beautiful," I murmured fervently.

My father nodded. Yes, it was beautiful, and also so childlike. No heavy satin or matronly draped décolletage for Sarah, but white organdy with a full skirt and a tiny waist, and a small round collar like the collar on a schoolgirl's blouse. The crown for her veil was also no crown, but a round little white brim, like the brim of a child's Breton. How young she looked, how young she insisted on looking, as if *her* marriage would never test and age her. Clara, murmuring to herself, considering, wrenched the waist around, smoothed down the front, and Sarah put out a hand to his secretary-desk to steady herself. Inside the top drawer was the new lifetime contract that the president had offered to him on Friday. He had not mentioned it to anyone because he had not wanted to dilute the happiness of Sarah's wedding day with a different kind of happiness. But he knew the document by heart already, and had signed it with a flourish. It had no fine print, no hidden clauses, no mysterious addenda. It merely, from that day forth, made him rabbi of Congregation Ezrath Israel, "The Actors Temple," for the rest of his life, and, if anything should happen to him, took care of Clara. Ducking his head, he quickly swiped at his eyes under his glasses. " 'He shall never repent that he sowed tears,' " he thought, " 'who shall bring home his sheaves in joy.' "

* * *

My mother wept, my father actually danced. But first there was the ceremony itself, which went by in a blur. It was strange coming into the crowded shul and not finding my father on the bima, but there was the cantor instead, waiting for him. The choir, stationed up in the Ladies Balcony, was humming a Hebrew melody, sounding like an organ since organs themselves were forbidden. Suddenly, the word to be still was passed along from row to row. Then came a friend of Sandy's, his best man, walking down the aisle as if he were looking for a seat. Then Sandy, sandwiched in between two aged parents—he was a change-of-life baby—smiling as if he had been arrested by mistake. A swell of voices. Mildred, transformed into the maid of honor, in blue chiffon, headed with small steps toward the altar, shaky bouquet held in both hands. The voices of the choir soared, the cantor's with them. All heads turned once more. And there was Sookie, the bride, *our* bride, in between my father and mother, my father in his long black robes, grinning from ear to ear. Angels sang. Sookie, all veiled and misted over in white, looked like an angel. Sandy, in his brown fedora, waiting on the bima, looked like Sandy. I wondered if it was the same hat I sat on the day it all began. "Oh, Easy," I whispered, tears streaming down my face. He squeezed my hand. I noticed that on the other side of him, he was squeezing Julia's.

Afterward, the rest of us headed for the Hotel Edison on foot, the bride and groom and parents in a limousine, as befitted their station. A limousine I hoped hadn't been provided by the Riverside Memorial Chapel. In the Sun

Room, a band was already playing lustily, people were dancing, and there was an elaborate buffet on a long table, featuring, among other items, a large red lobster. The entering wedding party stopped and stared at it. It wasn't from Trotsky's and it wasn't real, just something the Sun Room staff had thoughtfully provided as an extra fillip. My father, sighing, signaled to an uncomprehending waiter to take it away, and then, dressed in his cutaway and striped pants, headed for the dais where we were all to sit, and stopped the music to say kiddush over the wine. The music started up again, and Sandy and Sookie headed out onto the floor to dance. Easy cut in on them, then Yossie. Sandy was dancing with his stout sister. "Cut in on them, Uncle, go ahead," Easy said. "Don't be foolish." "Go ahead." Easy gave him a little nudge. My father took a few steps in place with a laughing Sookie. "Daddy's dancing!" I cried. "Daddy's dancing!" My mother took a look and dissolved in tears. I headed for the bar where I ordered a cocktail with a cherry in it. It was sweet and I knocked it back like a schnapps, then had another which I sipped more slowly, then another.

"How many of those Manhattans have you had already, Honey?" Ernie asked.

"I don't know. Three or four."

"I think you better eat something," Ernie said.

"Don't be silly," I said, nibbling at a piece of icing from the tall, tiered wedding cake.

A handsome young man materialized beside me. "Who are you?" he asked.

"The bride's sister. Who are you?"

"The groom's friend."

"If you're a doctor, I hate doctors."

"Maybe I can change your mind. Come on, let's dance."

We whirled about on the floor, I following as Sookie had taught me. Sandy's eyes widened as we swept past him. Big Sarah threw back her head and laughed, nudging Harry. I ignored my young cousins who had started to wave at me from the kiddie table.

"My name's Marty, by the way. What's yours?"

"Honey."

"Sweetheart, I asked you what your name was."

Did it have to be Anna at a time like this?

"Ann!" I cried, inspired. *"Ann!"*

"Okay, I heard you the first time." He held me closer. "How old are you, by the way?"

"Seventeen," I murmured with my eyes closed, lying as Tippy had taught me.

"My God, that's young."

A break in the music interrupted us. We sauntered back to the bar, where I turned from ordering another Manhattan to find him gone. He was talking to Sandy and looking as if he had just had a fit of apoplexy. So much for doctors. I sipped my Manhattan and then joined the lively Russian *sher* being danced in the center of the floor. We were all in a circle, dashing in and out, round and round, as the clarinets whirled. Big Sarah, hair redder than ever, black dress gleaming with gold sequins, lifted her long skirts, stepped lively with her pretty little feet, and excelled. Yossie crossed his arms, tried a *kasatske*, and fell on his behind. Sandy's mother, an elegant little Russian type of lady, twirled about waving her handkerchief. Anita and her husband skipped in circles with their arms linked. And meanwhile, people kept going back and forth stuffing envelopes with money in them into Sandy's pockets. And

Sookie had taken off her veil—why? I would have kept it on forever—and become herself.

Hours passed or minutes. I became embittered about the young doctor and determined to find him and tell him off, starting with, "Frankly, my dear, I don't give a damn." But he wasn't there anymore. Neither, for that matter, was most anybody.

"Come on, Honey," Easy said, lifting a Manhattan from my hand. "Time to go home."

"No. I don't want to. Where's everybody?"

"They've gone home too. See, the musicians are packing up."

"Sookie! I have to say good-bye to Sookie! Where's Sookie?"

"On her honeymoon," Easy said gently, taking me by the arm.

As we passed the huge wedding cake on the buffet table, I tried to grab a big hunk of it and stuff it in my mouth. But Easy took that out of my hand too.

"What did you do that for? It's delicious."

"It's plaster," Easy said.

I cried all the way back in the taxi, and when I got home I cried some more, dozing in between on the living-room sofa where I had flopped when we came in. When I woke up for the last time, it was still the same day, only more like yesterday than tomorrow. Easy and my father were playing chess at the inlaid table, my mother was mumbling over the *Forward*—Mildred, she told me, had gone out with one of the doctors—and Julia was practicing her choral reading in the dining room. "Come down to Kew in *lilac* time, in *lilac* time, in *lilac* time," Julia said urgently. "Come down to Kew in *lilac* time. It isn't far from London." Where Yossie was, nobody ever had any idea. It suddenly dawned on me for the first time that the only person who wasn't coming home, who would never come home again, was Sookie.

"*Shoch!*" my father cried triumphantly, and as Easy laughed and cleared away the chess pieces, went to ease himself in Cathrael's chair. I wished it were that morning and that we were back in Central Park and Sookie was rowing us around the lake. I could not take it in that this was never again to be.

"Honey," Easy said to cheer me up, "do you know how to make a Venetian blind?"

"No."

"Poke his eyes out."

"Oh, *Easy!*" I wailed.

My father in his chair, chin in hand, was also thinking of Sarah's wedding, but in another vein entirely. He was thinking that the cantor had a beautiful voice. His Kol Nidre could tear your heart out. And he was a jolly man besides, from the Ukraine like Clara, but with Big Sarah's readiness to laugh. It would be nice to have such a man as a personal assistant, with Ernie and Anita to handle the rest of it. Closer to home, he was also thinking that from one husband could come others, for Mildred, for Julia, even for me if I ever pulled myself together and stopped trying to show the boys how smart I was. Yosel, if he enlisted, as he was threatening to do practically every day now, might find some nice Orthodox girl overseas, and—who knew?—if the war went on as it was, eventually the United States Army might be asking for chaplains. Meanwhile, it wouldn't hurt for a rabbi with a lifetime contract—he didn't have to be in Cleveland—to consider collecting his sermons.

"Channele," he said, walking over to his desk, "stop crying for a minute and type this up."

I glanced at the folded sheet of paper he had handed me, notes for something:

The Midrash tells us that when God was deciding whether to create Man, he called his ministering angels to him for advice. Immediately there was an argument. Some of them said, "Create him," and some of them said, "Don't do it." Love said, "Yes, he will be loving." Peace said, "No, he will be full of strife." Righteousness said, "He will perform deeds of righteousness." And Truth said, "But he will be full of falsehood." So what did the Holy One, blessed be He, do? He threw Truth out of Heaven. Because Truth, He said, was a liar.

"Daddy—Truth was a *liar*?"

He looked over my shoulder. "So fix it up a little. Also put in something about Intolerance."

The Army wouldn't take him this time, either. He was overage and, as they pointed out, had a wife and children. So he settled for raising a great deal of money for the war effort, went to Washington to try to get Roosevelt to help the Jews, accepted testimonial plaques and scrolls, sent cigarettes overseas, invited the chorus boys from Winged Victory *home for shabbos, hired the cantor as an assistant, and got to Florida. V-E Day he celebrated quietly, sitting by an open window in his bedroom, shredding the pages of a telephone book and thoughtfully watching the pieces flutter to the street.*

We all did get married, with my father performing our wedding ceremonies. But long after we had moved away, Forty-seventh Street continued with its own changes and adventures and I kept hearing stories in a very familiar vein. Art Carney had come to my father for Hebrew lessons when he was about to play Mayor Briscoe of Dublin, Debbie Reynolds wanted my father and a priest to marry her to Eddie Fisher. The minyans were now assisted by dragooned waiters from Howard Johnson's and the congregation acquired a fellow named Crooked Dollar Moishe. At one benefit Harry Belafonte, unbuttoned to the waist, put his leg up on a stool and sang to a large guitar, followed by Frank Sinatra, who had long been an annual sensation. My own last vivid theatrical memory of my father is of seeing him with two of the Three Stooges. Only two, because only two were Jewish, the wild-haired one being a Polish Catholic. They had come to the synagogue that evening, Moe and Curly, to say kaddish for one of their parents, and when services were over, my father graciously ushered them out along with the rest of the congregation and locked up. Then the three of them started down Forty-seventh Street in the dusk. I lingered behind to watch them. It was a marvelous sight. One Stooge on one side, one Stooge on the other, and my father in the middle.

When my father died, in 1959, my mother woke from the drugged sleep the fight doctor had put her in, and got up to lay a square little black funeral dress on the empty bed beside her. "My king is dead," she said to Julia and me. "My friend." The next day Forty-seventh Street did him great honor and put hooded caps on all the parking me-

ters. The cops were out in full force, including the ones who hadn't been so helpful about the tap dancing from the rehearsal hall, and the street was clogged with bystanders. Inside, the synagogue was packed too, all the downstairs and also the Ladies Balcony jammed with people. I remember looking up and seeing nice Mrs. Williams, the widow of Singing Sam, the Barbasol man. Some strange rabbi kept saying, "Gut shabbos, Beril," and George Jessel delivered the eulogy dressed in a cutaway. On our way out, a lady clutched my arm and explained through tears why she hadn't been able to get out the whole membership. I said I understood and that my father would have too. Which was so. She was from AGVA, of which my father had been chaplain, and the missing members, thank God, were working in the Catskills. The funeral service at the cemetery was long and very Orthodox, and then we went back to my parents' house on Fifty-fourth Street right off Broadway, and sat shiva for seven days, in stockinged feet, on little wooden stools, mirrors covered up, eating around the clock, or so it seemed, in between visitors, while the present shammos scurried around as the old one had, trying to round up ten people for a minyan so that we could have the honor and respect, as a rabbi's family, of saying kaddish at home instead of having to go out. Though there was always that old nagging question of whether the shammos had caught them inside the synagogue saying kaddish for parents of their own, or nabbed them walking down Forty-seventh Street minding their own business.

Which, as they say in show biz, just about wraps it up. Except that Variety's obituary called my father "hep" and also I had one last little episode of my own, a year later, when I dropped by the synagogue on the anniversary of

my father's death, standing in the back to go ostenta-
tiously unrecognized. It wasn't really too bad. A fair number of people in the congregation, the familiar service, the
cantor up there on the red-carpeted bima, as if my father
hadn't been able to show up that evening, or would come
back in a few minutes. But something else was missing,
something that left me terribly heavy-hearted. We had the
words, but not the music. Then the service was over and
the congregation filed out and it was okay again. Because
the last one down the aisle was a midget.